CHOOSE YOURSELF

A 12-week Journey to Becoming the God of Your Own Heart

Stacie Aamon Yeldell
MA, MT-BC, AVPT

AMÖNTRA

DISCOVERING ONENESS

Choose Yourself
A 12-week Journey to Becoming
the God of Your Own Heart

Written by Stacie Aamon Yeldell,
MA, MT-BC, AVPT

Edited by Brady Hahn

Cover, workbook design and Illustrations By Keva Epale

Back cover, Photo Stacie Aamon Yeldell © Petra Kovacs

Amontra Music and Wellness, LLC
5551 Hollywood Blvd, #1245
Hollywood, CA 90028
www.weareamontra.com

ISBN: 979-8-218-26072-9
United States of America
August, 2023

Contents

WELCOME

MY STORY
FROM ABANDONMENT
TO HEALING

Welcome! My name is Stacie Aamon Yeldell, the founder of Amöntra, a consulting company based in Los Angeles, California. I am an award-winning vocalist, speaker, and music psychotherapist with over 15 years of experience in mental health treatment.

I have facilitated and treated over ten thousand individuals using therapeutic mindfulness practices in workplaces, retreats, treatment centers, and universities all across the country.

This workbook is for anyone who's been told, "you have to love yourself before anyone else can love you" and grimaced in response to it. This workbook is for anyone who, like me, has found the concept of self-care and self-love to be elusive and fleeting.

This workbook is a map to finding the answers that are planted within you.

This workbook will help you establish a ritual of daily communion with yourself - a communion to become the God of your own heart. Not only will this make you impervious to external validation and the incessant need to be loved or adored by another, but you will become a magnet to those who are able to meet you at the higher vibration.

And I am delighted to share it with you.

*For those constant "gardeners"
who have been toiling and
weeding the garden of life
only to find themselves repeating
patterns that are ancient
and maybe even beyond
this life or beyond this time...*

This is for you.

I began my recovery journey from abandonment to healing almost 20 years ago, with the help of a kick-ass therapist and Alanon (the 12-step program created for people who have been impacted by another person's alcoholism). I was under the impression that I'd had a nice childhood.

On the surface I was a cheerful kid, boisterous and creative. Sure, my dad drank, but I grew up with two loving parents who were physically present. As a young recording artist, my parents had always supported my dreams, driving me back and forth to rehearsals and performances, paying for outfits, producers and recording studio costs.

As an adult, I sought the advice from teachers, healers and psychics, yet, I still felt something was unsettled within me. Following a break-up with my childhood sweetheart, mysterious internal wounds that lay hidden for decades were exposed.

Working with a therapist, I learned that what I was experiencing was a form of "abandonment" - and that these "episodes" I experienced over the years - panic, anxiety, dizziness, derealization - were symptoms of *relational trauma**, a legitimate and diagnosable form of PTSD.

I was stunned. In all of the therapy and healing sessions I had attended over the years, no one had ever categorized my abandonment issues - let alone identified them as *trauma*. This sense of validation and relief sparked a gradual release from the hurt and shame I'd been carrying.

Somewhat synchronistically, I had just begun somatic trauma therapy training at an integrative treatment center where I was working at the time. In the first lecture, they explained the importance of psychoeducation. We were implored to educate our clients on the true nature of trauma, how it's intricately connected to the nervous system and how despite years of talk therapy, it can still remain very active in our unconscious.

Most importantly, we learned that re-experiencing a trauma such as abandonment isn't the fault of the client and that stabilization is required before trauma can be processed.

I started creating practices, activities and rituals that felt supportive and I made a vow to engage in at least three practices a day. Days turned into weeks, turned into months.

What began as a mandatory tool to survive, transformed into a necessary tool to thrive! I learned how to connect with my own heart and inner knowing - and now you can too!

About
The Workbook

MEETING YOUR OWN

CORE NEEDS

SPOILER ALERT

There are no magic pills here!

If magic pills were really a thing, I probably wouldn't have created this workbook! It can feel strange to embark on the revolutionary mission of meeting our own core *needs*. This can be especially true if, like me, you were the "little nurturer" in your family or if giving to others feels more easy and natural than receiving from others. There may even be downright resistance to practicing this level of self-care. Unconsciously you may procrastinate, create distractions or get bored.

If you experience any of this, guess what? You are not to blame. Most of us have memories of books, songs and of course, fairytales that promised a knight in shining armor that would arrive on a horse and magically meet *all of our needs*. We are programmed to believe that the answers and support we need exists outside ourselves - instead of seeking the answers from within ourselves.

The good news is, identifying and meeting your *core needs* is a practice. Similar to yoga, this isn't about doing a handstand or contorting oneself into a pretzel. In fact, it's not about perfection at all.

As you identify and meet your core needs through your *self-devotional practices*, over time, you will experience the transformative healing elixir, the elusive state known as "self-love"-not as merely a concept, but as a verb.

ABOUT THIS

WORKBOOK

This workbook contains 12-weeks of guided content. As you prepare to take this journey, I invite you to dedicate a journal or note app space for the **daily exercises** contained in this workbook. These practices will require just 15 minutes a day starting with 5 minutes of *grounding*, followed by 5 minutes of journaling, and ending with a 5 minute evening reflection.

Gradually, your morning grounding and journaling practice will increase to 20 minutes, then 30 minutes, with the 5 minute evening reflection remaining the same over the 12-week course.

This 12-week journey is divided into 3 modules, including...

WEEKLY THEMES
Each week you will explore a different theme highlighting key behaviors, belief systems and emotional patterns. These themes are intended to be guideposts, helping you to chart your course and center your focus, one step at a time.

INSPIRING AFFIRMATIONS
More than a motivational quote, an affirmation helps to "seal" your *meditation* practice. I am a bit of a "post-it" gal, so I like to place affirmative statements in areas of my home where I will see it often (my bathroom mirror, refrigerator, or the front door, etc.).

In the appendix, you will find additional resources to support your journey.

THE AMÖNTRA "ALL THE FEELS" LIST
A list of words to help you better describe your feelings during your daily journaling exercises and in your everyday life!

A LIST OF TERMS
Detailed explanations of some of the terms used throughout the workbook.

DAILY EXERCISES

MORNING GROUNDING

Meditation:
Each module will have
a dedicated guided morning
meditation that you can do
seated anywhere you like.

Journaling:
New journal prompts will be
provided each week that you
can record in your journal
or note app.

EVENING REFLECTION

At the end of each day,
prompts are provided to
encourage you to reflect
on the day in your journal
or note app - it only takes
5 minutes!

Getting Started

SETTING YOUR DEVOTIONAL PRACTICES

This workbook encourages a holistic, body, mind, spirit approach to healing. Most of us have heard of Gary Chapman's 1992 book, "The Five Love Languages", a guide for couples that outlines five ways in which we express and experience love for someone else.

What if you were to repurpose this concept by directing that energy "inward", essentially tethering your "untethered soul" back to you? Instead of focusing on a partner and how they feel most loved, this workbook will show you how to turn the lens on yourself. The Self-Devotion Checklist is designed to help identify the habits, self-care practices, and rituals that make you feel loved.

5 KEYS AREAS OF SELF-DEVOTION

Meditation
Each day, you will practice the activation of your awareness, cultivation of inner stillness, and observation of your thoughts, with curiosity and compassion. As you gain more dominion over your mind, you will gain more dominion over your thoughts.

Journaling
After your meditation, you will capture your insights and revelations through a daily journaling practice. This will deepen your self-understanding and allow you to connect key areas of growth over the next 12-weeks and beyond!

Movement
You are encouraged to move for 20 minutes or more a day. Movement releases tension and stress and increases serotonin levels in the brain, thus boosting your mood. Movement can include exercises such as yoga, walking, dancing or hiking.

Nourishment
As a practice, daily nourishment provides sustenance, promotes harmony, and an overall sense of well-being. This can include preparing/eating whole fresh foods, getting a massage, taking a salt bath, or spending time in the sun, or in nature.

Create Your Own Devotion
Ask yourself, what sparks your creativity? This is a chance to discover other ways to shower yourself with devotion and fill up each day!

THE SELF-DEVOTION CHECKLIST

Review the following list for inspiration. Using your dedicated journal or workbook, write down the practices and rituals that you currently use in your daily/weekly life. Make note of any new ideas you can incorporate into your practice of self-devotion within each of the 5 categories.
Note: items marked with an asterisk "*" are provided in this workbook.

Meditation

○ Walking Meditation
○ Visual Meditation/Grounding Practice*
○ *Point Of Focus Meditation*
○ Breathwork
○ Body Scanning
○ Sound Meditation

○ Other _____

Journaling

○ Prompted Journaling*
○ Morning Pages
○ Visual Journaling (art, collage, etc.)
○ Bullet Journaling
○ Dictated Journaling (voice recorder)

○ Other _____

Movement

○ Biking
○ Yoga
○ Strength Training
○ Nature Walk
○ Dance
○ Gym

○ Other _____

Nourishment

○ Singing
○ Hobby _____
○ Culinary Delight/Eating
○ Reading   ○ Sunbathing
○ Bath (salt/bubbles)
○ Aromatherapy/Essential Oils
○ Bodywork (facial/mask/massage)
○ Ritual: Honoring A Cycle (moon, equinox, menstrual, etc.)
○ Creative Expression
   o Writing (book, essay, song, etc.)
   o Decorate Your Altar
   o Cooking
   o Art (draw, paint, sketch)
○ Other _____

Other

○ Volunteering
○ Attending A Concert/Event
○ Taking A Class
○ Listening To Podcast
○ Talking To Friend/Trusted Advisor
○ Hanging With Friend(s)/Family
○ Day Trip/Adventure

○ Other _____

Weekly Grounding Practices

CALLING BACK YOUR POWER

WELCOME TO MODULE ONE!

In these four weeks, we are building and reinforcing a foundation for your daily practice. Our goal is to start to delicately regain dominion over the mind, by revealing debilitating unconscious belief systems that can distract us from the present moment. We will explore tools to regulate your emotions in a healthy way, and begin the process of calling back your power from outdated programming about love, loving, and what it means to be loved.

WEEK 1	**Rumination vs. Observation - Attention As Currency**
WEEK 2	**Contraction vs. Expansion - The Key To Emotional Regulation**
WEEK 3	**Insourcing vs. Outsourcing - What Are You Plugged Into?**
WEEK 4	**Fantasy vs. Reality - The Myth Of "Being Chosen"**

Daily Exercises

This module will focus on establishing a 15-minute grounding practice.

Each morning, you will complete the same 5-minute meditation throughout the module. Each week, you will have a new affirmation, morning and evening journaling prompts, as well as a checklist to track your progress.

I encourage you to set aside 15 minutes each day, 10 minutes in the morning to meditate and journal, and 5 minutes for reflection in the evening to gain the most benefit from the practice.

5 MINUTE MEDITATION

You can utilize this recording to guide you in your grounding practice.

🎧 LISTEN HERE

Take a seat and let's begin!

If comfortable or appropriate, close your eyes, or simply turn your gaze downwards.

In your mind's eye, trace a mental circle around yourself, as if you were able to visualize where your energetic field begins and ends. Experiment with arm's length, then tracing the circle farther out. Notice what feels safest for you. **This is your space – this is your** *energetic boundary.*

Bring your attention to the bottoms of the feet. Begin to sense the connection between your feet and the earth. Then, in your mind's eye, draw a line of energy from the bottoms of your feet into the center of the earth. **This is a fantastic opportunity to give yourself permission to activate the imagination.**

Sense this line of energy moving from the bottom of the feet, through the floorboards, the layers of rock and sediment underneath you, until it reaches the core of the planet. Once you are able to experience this connection, allow the line of energy to expand, perhaps forming into sturdy roots.

Allow the imagery to emerge in your mind's eye, naturally. Perhaps, another image comes to mind: a waterfall or rays of light. As your feet begin to ground into the earth, allow any remaining tension, stress or rigidity to release down through the grounding roots at the base of the feet.

Stay here, breathing and releasing, until you begin to feel calm, steady and centered.

Then, bring your attention to the base of the spine, or the point of connection between your body and the seat of your chair. Then, in your mind's eye, draw a line of energy from your seat into the center of the earth. When you sense this connection, watch the line of energy to expand into a *grounding cord,* widening to the width of your chair. Perhaps, you can visualize yourself sitting on a Redwood tree stump, or allow any other imagery that resonates with you to naturally emerge.

23

Postulate a chair or seat in the center of the mind. **Bring your attention to this space, this room behind your eyes and then allow it to rest in this chair or seat. This is your "*perch*."**

Begin to notice this shift in perspective, almost as if you are able to simply observe your emotions, thoughts and feelings from this viewpoint. Then, ground the mind by visualizing a line of energy extending from the center of the mind into the center of the planet. Allow this line of energy to expand and release any tension, stress or racing thoughts down through the mind and into the center of the earth. Continue to breathe.

You may stay here as long as you like.

**THE MEDITATION IS COMPLETE.
YOU ARE NOW CONNECTED!**

WEEK 1

RUMINATION vs. OBSERVATION

This week's goal is to provide you with tools to practice observing your thought patterns without judgment.

Essentially, you are practicing the art of paying attention to your own thoughts and actions to observe where and how you spend your time.

RUMINATION vs. OBSERVATION

ATTENTION AS CURRENCY

THEME OF THE WEEK

If your focus was a currency, what would you pay attention to? Energy flows where attention goes. This week explores the phenomena of focus and how our emotional states and overall experience is dictated by whatever we choose to "pay attention" to.

Here is a question for you: If your attention was currency, what would you pay attention to? Think about this. It may sound like a trick question, but if you look beyond the play on words, you will discover a well of truth. Arguably, our "attention" may be our hottest commodity.

In a world where social media has captured the attention of the free world - and a handful of social media platform pioneers are rebelling, forming coalitions and have banned their own children from using facebook - it is clear to see when viewed through the proper lens that attention = control. In essence, whatever you are paying attention to has control over you in that moment.

For example, if you are focused on the present moment - what you have, what is working, how far you have come, how much you have to look forward to - then you will most likely begin to feel expansive and happy. This is why gratitude lists can be immensely therapeutic.

Conversely, when you focus on the *absence* - what isn't working, what he or she said, why you aren't where you want to be, how hard life is - then guaranteed, you will begin to feel contracted (ashamed, depressed, defeated, hopeless) and potentially be more prone to sadness, depression, and anger, or just a general sense of "shittyness".

The mind is simple. It just wants SOMETHING to obsess about.

So, why not feed it healthy and wholesome material? It doesn't mean we ignore the "bad". This is about reclaiming our dominion over the mind and asserting our power as its owner. We are standing up for ourselves and saying essentially, "I will not sell myself short by paying attention to that which does not serve my highest good."

I am showered
in total self-love
and self-compassion
as I shed old patterns
completely.
This is a judgment
- free zone!

DAILY EXERCISES

 MORNING & EVENING | Repeat each of the following elements daily for one week.

MORNING GROUNDING
Start each morning by reading or listening to the 5-minute meditation.

MORNING JOURNALING
In your dedicated journal, take 5 minutes to respond to one or all of the following prompts:

1. What did you notice about your "perch"? Describe the room you discovered, or if you are feeling artsy, sketch it. How does it feel being in your perch today?

2. How did your energetic boundary feel today? What do you notice when you pay attention to its presence? For example, does it have a shape, a size or color?

3. During the meditation, were there any thoughts that competed for your attention? If yes, was there one that stood out to you?

4. Self-Devotional Practices
Movement: I will move my body by...
Nourishment: I will feel nourished by...
Your Own: To spark my creativity, I will...

EVENING REFLECTION
At the end of each day, take five minutes to reflect in your journal using one or more of the following prompts:

1. Was there a time today when you found yourself *ruminating* or did something occupy your attention for more time than it needed to? If yes, what were you focusing on?

2. Was there a time today when you were able to shift your focus intentionally from a distraction or negative thought back to your perch or a place of non-attachment?

3. Knowing this, what intention would you like to set for tomorrow?

Validate and congratulate yourself before you drift off to sleep.

 WEEK IN REVIEW | On the last day of your week, take 5 minutes to reflect in your journal.

WITHOUT JUDGMENT, REVIEW YOUR WEEKLY TRACKER. How many days were you able to implement your self devotional practices? Which practices felt the most balancing? How can you adjust them for the week ahead?

REFLECTING BACK ON THE WEEK, WHAT DID YOU OBSERVE/LEARN FROM THE EXERCISES THIS WEEK? How has this method of returning to your perch helped you? Are you noticing more examples of synchronicity and flow?

SELF-DEVOTION WEEKLY TRACKER

WEEK _____

This is a judgment free zone. Take a moment to record your journey through the daily exercises and devotional practices. Place a check in the box for each exercise you have completed.

Daily Exercises

DAYS OF THE WEEK

	SU	M	T	W	T	F	S
MORNING GROUNDING							
Meditation	○	○	○	○	○	○	○
Journaling	○	○	○	○	○	○	○
EVENING REFLECTION	○	○	○	○	○	○	○

Self-Devotional Practices

MOVEMENT _____	○	○	○	○	○	○	○
NOURISHMENT _____	○	○	○	○	○	○	○
YOUR OWN DEVOTION _____	○	○	○	○	○	○	○

Notes

WEEK 2

CONTRACTION vs. EXPANSION

This week's goal is to provide tools that will allow you to increase your awareness of fluctuating states of emotions.

Instead of self-medicating or being like the leaf on the breeze - blowing wherever your emotions take you - this week will assist you in mastering your emotions through healthy emotional regulation techniques.

CONTRACTION vs. EXPANSION

THE KEY TO EMOTIONAL REGULATION

THEME OF THE WEEK

In a world plagued with mental health crises, such as depression and anxiety – and a society obsessed with feeding us myriad ways to **"feel good"**, it is more important than ever to master the fine art of *emotional regulation*. The topic might seem complicated, but here is a simple question: **how would your reality change if we could contextualize your emotional life through the lens of two distinct categories: contraction or expansion?**

The psychologist Carl Jung theorized that "...when an inner situation is not made conscious, it happens outside as fate. That is to say, when the individual remains undivided and does not become conscious of his inner opposite, the world must act out the conflict and be torn into opposing halves." In other words, you will be living in a contracted state of *dysregulation* (Henriques, 2017).

Being in a contracted state is similar to what Jung described as the *"shadow"* self. This is the side of the psyche you may block, repress, or defend against because it could be threatening and antithetical to who you wish to be. Being in an expanded state simply means that you are likely able to experience a wide range of pleasant emotions, without necessarily denying or medicating the experience of contractive emotions.

Expansion and contraction is an integral aspect of transformation and growth. This motion is actually life-giving – it is the same movement required to birth a baby. Similarly to this birthing process, the more we contract and expand emotionally, the more we dilate, ie: create space to move into - and hold - more expansive emotional states of being.

When I first discovered Nene (the name I gave my shadow self), she was nothing like me. She wasn't spiritual or strong. She didn't feel any kind of connection to God, the Universe or anything like it. Nene was selfish, unruly and constantly flirted with the past. She was a saboteur - reckless, selfish, and scared. She was the reigning queen of my darkest days.

In a failed effort to silence her, I self-medicated. Then, foolishly, I thought that assuming a healthier lifestyle would be enough to get rid of her. But instead of peace, I found myself at war with her. I would eventually discover in therapy that "Nene" was merely an out-picturing of the wounded child — an aspect of myself that was too painful for me to face.

This story highlights the importance of embracing our shadow self - and the complex emotions that come along with it. The key is to validate the contractive feeling, rather than labeling it "bad". If we attempt to move into an expansive state without "doing the work" of fully feeling the contractive emotion, then we risk doing what is called "spiritual bypassing"- this is a "tendency to use spiritual ideas and practices to sidestep or avoid facing unresolved emotional issues, psychological wounds, and unfinished developmental tasks" (Fosella & Welwood, 2011).

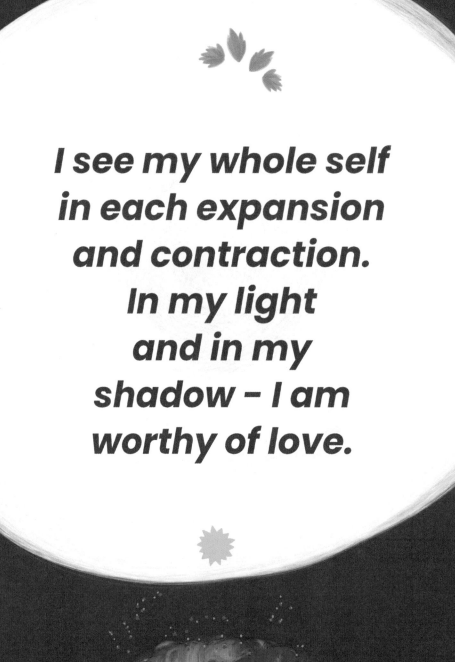

**I see my whole self
in each expansion
and contraction.
In my light
and in my
shadow – I am
worthy of love.**

DAILY EXERCISES

MORNING & EVENING | Repeat each of the following elements daily for one week.

MORNING GROUNDING
Start each morning by reading or listening to the 5-minute meditation.

MORNING JOURNALING
In your dedicated journal, take 5 minutes to respond to one or all of the following prompts:

1. Name one way you could have used your Self-Devotion tools to regulate your emotions and return to your "perch."

2. Think of a time when you felt fully *expanded*. Using the "All The Feels" guide, name how you felt in that moment. Which devotional practices give you that same feeling?

3. Think of a time when you were emotionally *contracted*. Using the "All The Feels" guide, which emotion(s) did you feel in that moment? What habits or actions did you use to soothe your emotions?

4. Self-Devotional Practices
Movement: I will move my body by...
Nourishment: I will feel nourished by...
Your Own: To spark my creativity, I will...

EVENING REFLECTION
At the end of each day, take five minutes to reflect in your journal using one or more of the following prompts:

1. Reflecting on the day, when did you emotionally contract? What word(s) would you use to describe how you felt? Note the moments, events or people that contributed to that feeling. What did you do to regulate your emotions?

2. Note the moments you felt a sense of expansion. What sensations did you experience? Where are these sensations located in your body?

3. Thinking of an example from today (or a previous instance that comes to mind), name one way you could have used your self devotion tools to regulate your emotions and return to your "perch."

Validate and congratulate yourself before you drift off to sleep.

WEEK IN REVIEW | On the last day of your week, take 5 minutes to reflect in your journal.

WITHOUT JUDGMENT, REVIEW YOUR WEEKLY TRACKER. How many days were you able to implement your self devotional practices? Which practices felt the most balancing? How can you adjust them for the week ahead?

REFLECTING BACK ON THE WEEK, WHAT DID YOU OBSERVE/LEARN FROM THE EXERCISES THIS WEEK? How has this method of returning to your perch helped you? Are you noticing more examples of synchronicity and flow?

SELF-DEVOTION WEEKLY TRACKER

WEEK _____

This is a judgment free zone. Take a moment to record your journey through the daily exercises and devotional practices. Place a check in the box for each exercise you have completed.

Daily Exercises

DAYS OF THE WEEK

	SU	M	T	W	T	F	S
MORNING GROUNDING							
Meditation	○	○	○	○	○	○	○
Journaling	○	○	○	○	○	○	○
EVENING REFLECTION	○	○	○	○	○	○	○

Self-Devotional Practices

	SU	M	T	W	T	F	S
MOVEMENT _____	○	○	○	○	○	○	○
NOURISHMENT _____	○	○	○	○	○	○	○
YOUR OWN DEVOTION _____	○	○	○	○	○	○	○

Notes

WEEK 3

INSOURCING vs. OUTSOURCING

This week, we will explore codependent tendencies to assist you in connecting to your own inner power source of strength.

This week's goal is to begin noticing what you are "plugged" into, as well as to identify potential energy leaks and other potentially unhealthy attachments.

INSOURCING vs. OUTSOURCING

WHAT ARE YOU PLUGGED INTO?

THEME OF THE WEEK

What does it mean to be *codependent?* Codependency is characterized by making extreme sacrifices for the needs of another, difficulty setting boundaries, feeling trapped in a relationship. In other words, it is when we "nurture the afflicted to the point where it is detrimental to our own health and wellbeing." (LaPoire, 1992).

Another way we may give away our power is by plugging into the outside world for our love and validation. This can be insidious and sneaky because this behavior may be unconscious, in other words, hidden from our view. We don't even realize we are doing it. The shift is subtle changes in your emotional state, a sense of feeling uneasy, or off balance. You may even feel like you are being emotionally pulled towards another person or story in your mind.

Unfortunately, we live in a society that encourages such entanglement - even some of the music that comprises the "soundtrack" of our everyday life is interwoven with pleas and proclamations, like "I can't breathe without you" and "I have nothing if I don't have you." How often do we consider the impact songs with codependent lyrics can have on our subconscious?

Another example is social media - how many times have you felt that jolt of enthusiasm when someone likes one of your photos? The subtle validation we glean from outside sources is seductive and can even become addictive. It's not that social media is "bad", but we want to be operating at our full power and potential. So it is within this module that we begin to become more aware of our "energy leaks," those places, spaces and individuals that slowly usurp our power.

Judith Orloff states: "Many of us instinctively want to take away another person's pain, especially a loved one, but that can be unhealthy for those who soak up their negative energy" (Orloff, 2018). This week, we will explore *etheric cords*. Similar to quantum entanglement, etheric cords or energy cords can be thought of as invisible links between you and another person, place or object that allow you to instantly affect one another.

When I feel myself reaching out, I call my attention and power back to my perch. I am whole and complete.

DAILY EXERCISES

 MORNING & EVENING | Repeat each of the following elements daily for one week.

MORNING GROUNDING
Start each morning by reading or listening to the 5-minute meditation.

MORNING JOURNALING
In your dedicated journal, take 5 minutes to respond to one or all of the following prompts:

1. During the meditation, did you sense any holes, leaks or cords? If yes, who are they with?

2. Select one cord today and name the person or story at the end of the chord. What is the *"agreement"* that is holding this cord in place? (Ex: "I will heal you in exchange for love" or "I will carry your pain because that is what love is").

3. How could you approach removing each of these emotional cords in your minds eye?

4. Self Devotional Practices
Movement: I will move my body by...
Nourishment: I will feel nourished by...
Your Own: To spark my creativity, I will...

EVENING REFLECTION
At the end of each day, take five minutes to reflect in your journal using one or more of the following prompts:

1. Reflecting on your day, who did you feel "plugged" into? Using the "All The Feels" list, what emotion describes the feeling(s) behind that connection?

2. Selecting one of the cords, imagine yourself gently releasing the cord from your body. What Does it feel like to let the attachment go? Repeat as necessary this week.

3. Knowing this, what intention would you like to set for tomorrow?

Validate and congratulate yourself before you drift off to sleep.

 WEEK IN REVIEW | On the last day of your week, take 5 minutes to reflect in your journal.

WITHOUT JUDGMENT, REVIEW YOUR WEEKLY TRACKER. How many days were you able to implement your self devotional practices? Which practices felt the most balancing? How can you adjust them for the week ahead?

REFLECTING BACK ON THE WEEK, WHAT DID YOU OBSERVE/LEARN FROM THE EXERCISES THIS WEEK? How has this method of returning to your perch helped you? Are you noticing more examples of synchronicity and flow?

SELF-DEVOTION WEEKLY TRACKER

WEEK _____

This is a judgment free zone. Take a moment to record your journey through the daily exercises and devotional practices. Place a check in the box for each exercise you have completed.

Daily Exercises

DAYS OF THE WEEK

	SU	M	T	W	T	F	S
MORNING GROUNDING							
Meditation	○	○	○	○	○	○	○
Journaling	○	○	○	○	○	○	○
EVENING REFLECTION	○	○	○	○	○	○	○

Self-Devotional Practices

MOVEMENT _____	○	○	○	○	○	○	○
NOURISHMENT _____	○	○	○	○	○	○	○
YOUR OWN DEVOTION _____	○	○	○	○	○	○	○

Notes

WEEK 4

FANTASY vs. REALITY

This week, we will explore, identify and dispel the myths of "being chosen" that lay burrowed deep inside of our subconscious mind.

The goal is to assist you in identifying the myriad of ways you may be placing your value outside of yourself and to continue to incorporate the fine art of self-validation (e.g., the practice of choosing yourself) into your daily practice.

FANTASY vs. REALITY

THE MYTH OF "BEING CHOSEN"

THEME OF THE WEEK

There are numerous ways we externalize our value:

- Believing in the age-old tale of falling in love and being rescued by Prince Charming.
- Working your fingers to the bone in hopes of a promotion, only to be overlooked by a superior.
- Enduring heart-crushing ostracization and subsequent isolation when rejected by a clique, sorority or other social group.

These are all examples of an unconscious externalization of our value.

In essence, many of us have been socialized to believe that we are only worthy of love, adoration, praise or acceptance if/when we are chosen by someone else.

Ever since I can remember, I longed to be "chosen." As a teenage rapper in the 90's - the golden-era of Hip-Hop - one of my favorite songs was EPMD's "Please Listen to My Demo." This tune illustrates the incredibly grueling process of trying to get your music heard by an aloof and elusive record exec, in the hopes of scoring a record deal.

I couldn't have imagined the ways in which this kind of thinking (or programming) would impact my artist self, as well as other areas of my life. As mentioned in the last week, if you give someone the power to *validate* you, you also give them the power to *invalidate* you.

Sayings like, "comparison is the thief of joy" and "compare equals despair" also speak to the harmful effects of comparing our chapter 4 to someone else's chapter 42. When you romanticize or idealize that dream job or dream relationship that someone else appears to have, you are buying into the myth that circumstances need to be "just so" in order for you to be happy.

Hinging your happiness on the happenings in your external world without shifting your internal reality is akin to the idiom of "rearranging the deck chairs on the Titanic." **The truth is, there is no outside person, place or thing that will guarantee sustainable joy.**

This week, we will step out of fantasy and into reality.

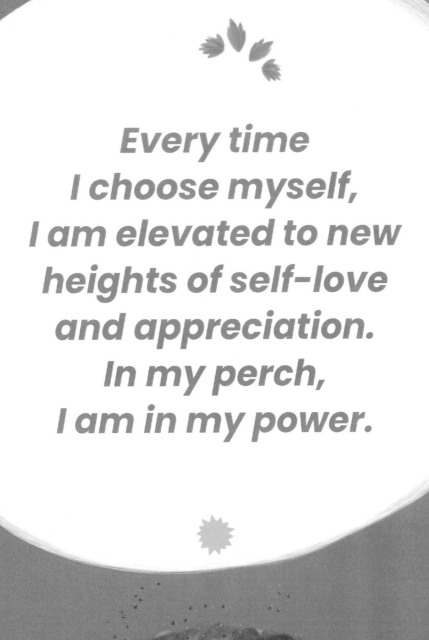

**Every time
I choose myself,
I am elevated to new
heights of self-love
and appreciation.
In my perch,
I am in my power.**

DAILY EXERCISES

MORNING & EVENING | Repeat each of the following elements daily for one week.

MORNING GROUNDING
Start each morning by reading or listening to the 5-minute meditation.

MORNING JOURNALING
In your dedicated journal, take 5 minutes to respond to one or all of the following prompts:

1. What beliefs, stories or myths did you hear in your childhood or adolescence regarding being "chosen" (ex: Prince Charming, a social group at school, an audition)?

2. Is there any area of your life where you are still waiting to be "chosen"? If yes, what story are you telling yourself?

3. Take time each day to create a playlist (7 songs) that make you feel expanded and empowered. Throughout the week, play these songs as a reminder of love for yourself.

4. Self-Devotional Practices
Movement: I will move my body by...
Nourishment: I will feel nourished by...
Your Own: To spark my creativity, I will...

EVENING REFLECTION
At the end of each day, take five minutes to reflect in your journal using one or more of the following prompts:

1. As you moved through your day, are there examples of when you noticed the tendency to externalize your value or worth?

2. What story/commentary or judgment did your mind weave around this circumstance? Knowing this, ask yourself, "is it true?"

3. Knowing this, what intention would you like to set for tomorrow?

Validate and congratulate yourself before you drift off to sleep.

WEEK IN REVIEW | On the last day of your week, take 5 minutes to reflect in your journal.

WITHOUT JUDGMENT, REVIEW YOUR WEEKLY TRACKER. How many days were you able to implement your self devotional practices? Which practices felt the most balancing? How can you adjust them for the week ahead?

REFLECTING BACK ON THE WEEK, WHAT DID YOU OBSERVE/LEARN FROM THE EXERCISES THIS WEEK? How has this method of returning to your perch helped you? Are you noticing more examples of synchronicity and flow?

SELF-DEVOTION WEEKLY TRACKER

WEEK _____

This is a judgment free zone. Take a moment to record your journey through the daily exercises and devotional practices.
Place a check in the box for each exercise you have completed.

Daily Exercises		DAYS OF THE WEEK						
		SU	M	T	W	T	F	S
MORNING GROUNDING								
Meditation		○	○	○	○	○	○	○
Journaling		○	○	○	○	○	○	○
EVENING REFLECTION		○	○	○	○	○	○	○

Self Devotional Practices

MOVEMENT _____	○	○	○	○	○	○	○
NOURISHMENT _____	○	○	○	○	○	○	○
YOUR OWN _____	○	○	○	○	○	○	○

Notes

MODULE 1 IN REVIEW

TAKE A MOMENT TO REFLECT ON YOUR JOURNEY SO FAR IN YOUR JOURNAL.
Without judgment, looking across your weekly tracker, how many days were you able to implement your self-devotional practices this month? What did you learn from adding these practices into your daily life?

REFLECTING BACK ON THE MONTH, WHAT ARE YOUR TOP LEARNINGS?
To close out the month, what are you most proud of and how can you celebrate all that you have accomplished thus far?

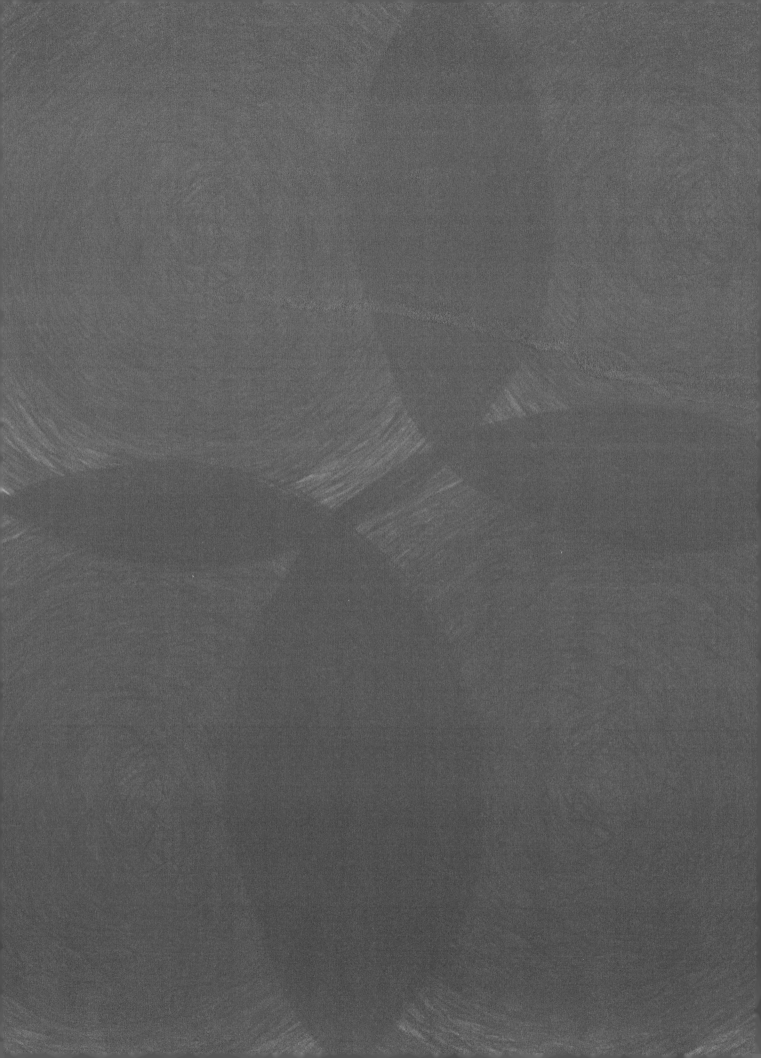

ANCHORING YOUR PRESENCE

WELCOME TO MODULE TWO!

Congratulations on completing the first module. By now, you have built a solid foundation and learned simple ways to hold your "space" and identify some of your mental and emotional patterns. In this next module, we will begin to identify and release self-victimization, learn to set and hold boundaries (that stick!), and step more intently into your power. You will deepen your understanding of what it means to be empathic, and cultivate forgiveness.

WEEK 5	**Tuning Into The Empath Within**
WEEK 6	**Setting Boundaries With Energy Vampires**
WEEK 7	**Recognizing The Lies We Tell Ourselves**
WEEK 8	**Cultivating Emotional Neutrality**

Daily Exercises

This module will focus on establishing a 25-minute grounding practice.

Building on the practice you established in Module One, the next four weeks will focus on adding 5 more minutes to your meditation practice. Each morning, you will complete this 10-minute meditation, morning and evening journaling prompts, as well as a checklist to track your progress.

I encourage you to set aside 25 minutes each day, 20 minutes in the morning to meditate and journal, and 5 minutes for reflection in the evening to gain the most benefit from the practice.

10 MINUTE MEDITATION

You can utilize this recording to guide you in your grounding practice.

🎧 LISTEN HERE

Take a seat and let's begin!

If comfortable or appropriate, close your eyes, or simply turn your gaze downwards.

In your mind's eye, trace a mental circle around yourself, as if you were able to visualize where your energetic field begins and ends. experiment with arm's length, then tracing the circle farther out. Notice what feels safest for you. **This is your *space* - your** energetic boundary.

Bring your attention to the bottoms of the feet. Begin to sense the connection between your feet and the earth. Then, in your mind's eye, draw a line of energy from the bottoms of your feet into the center of the earth. **This is a fantastic opportunity to give yourself permission to activate the imagination.**

Sense this line of energy moving from the bottom of the feet, through the floorboards, the layers of rock and sediment underneath you, until it reaches the core of the planet. Notice how you are able to experience this connection. Allow the line of energy to expand, perhaps forming into sturdy, hollow and strong roots.

Allow the imagery to emerge in your mind's eye, naturally. Perhaps, another image comes to mind: a waterfall or rays of light. As your feet begin to ground into the Earth, allow any remaining tension, stress or rigidity to release down through the grounding roots at the base of the feet.

Stay here, breathing and releasing, until you begin to feel steady, calm and centered.

Then, bring your attention to the base of the spine, or the point of connection between your body and the seat of your chair. Then, in your mind's eye, draw a line of energy from your seat into the center of the earth. When you sense this connection, watch the line of energy to expand into a grounding cord, widening to the width of your chair. Perhaps, you can visualize yourself sitting on a Redwood tree stump, or allow any other imagery that resonates with you to naturally emerge.

Postulate a chair or seat in the center of the mind. **Bring your attention to this space, this room behind your eyes and then allow it to rest in this chair or seat. This is your "perch".**

Begin to release any tension, stress or rigidity down through your feet or your seat and into the center of the Earth. **Lightly scan the body. If you sense any energy that isn't "yours" or that feels unfamiliar, notice what or who it may be connected to.**

If this energy is no longer serving you, then you can, as your own authority, adjust or void the *agreement* and then release this energy, with love and compassion.

If you sense an energetic cord and would like to remove it, then visualize yourself "voiding" the agreement. It could be helpful to visualize the person or situation. See the agreement and make the adjustments. You can even ask for support from your higher self to complete this agreement. Once those adjustments are made, visualize yourself removing the cord, gently.

If you do not sense any cords, great! Move on to the last step.

To close this practice, postulate a giant, bright, yellow sun over your head.

Imagine this sun pouring into the top of the head and filling in the spaces and places in the body that released tension. Feel the rejuvenating rays replenish your mind and body. Also, fill in any spaces where cords were removed.

Breathe and begin to feel the rejuvenating rays replenish your mind and body. Visualize yourself as a cup and allow this sun to pour in and fill you until you are full to overflowing.

Breathe and receive that *golden sun* into the feet, the ankles, into the knees and the legs. Go at your own pace. Fill in your seat, moving upwards into the solar plexus, then the heart. Allow the golden sun to move into the shoulders and down the arms and through the hands. Send the golden light upwards into the throne of the head, filling the center of the mind where you are seated on your Perch. Allow this golden sun to fill in every cell of your being. When you feel completely full of this golden light, begin to bring slight movement to the body and the hands. Stretch lightly.

When you feel completely ready and validated, you can open your eyes. You are welcome to close your daily meditation with this practice as an act of self-validation.

THE EXERCISE IS COMPLETE. YOU ARE CONNECTED!

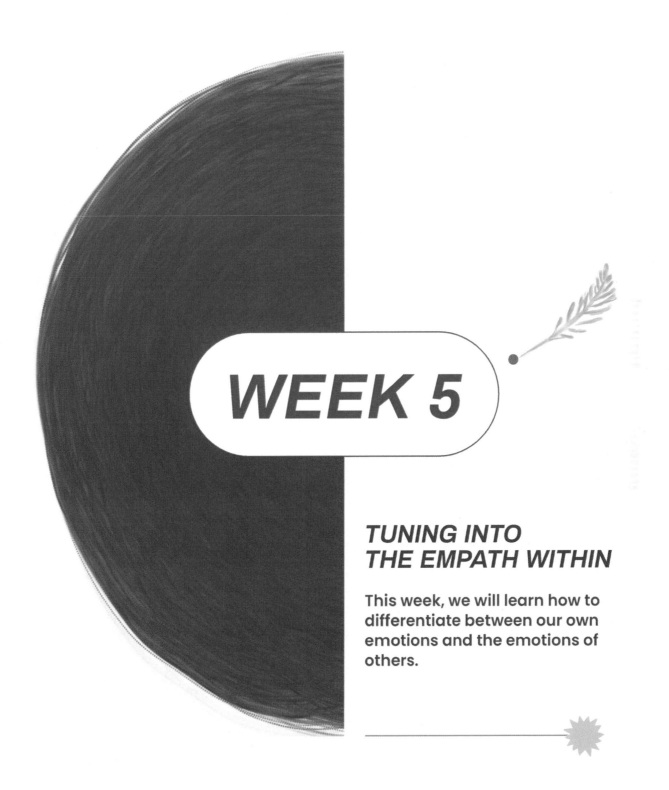

WEEK 5

TUNING INTO THE EMPATH WITHIN

This week, we will learn how to differentiate between our own emotions and the emotions of others.

TUNING INTO THE EMPATH WITHIN

Did you know, many of the feelings we experience are often not even our own? Think about this for a moment. How often have you been feeling happy or peaceful and then walked into a meeting or a party and had your entire mood shift?

Chances are, the fact that you were drawn to this workbook means you have strong empathetic traits. In general, most humans are sponges - absorbing the energy from our environment - and this is especially true for those of us who are sensitive *and* empathic.

An empath, sensitive or clairsentient person is someone who easily and effortlessly picks up the emotions and energy of a room or another person. It is a gift, really. Most of these people were "little nurturers" when they were children and oftentimes grow up to become teachers, counselors and healers. However, if you don't practice boundary setting and radical self-care, then this gift can begin to feel more like a curse.

Internalizing other people's emotions can feel like a deep connection, but in fact it is more like "debris" that gets caught in your energy field. As it accumulates over time it can result in making you feel tired, easily overwhelmed, and unable to regulate your emotions - which temporarily drowns out the subtle yet steady pulsing of the signal that is you and your truth.

In Module One, you had the opportunity to identify etheric cords. While the internalization of other people's emotions may be amplified by etheric cords, this type of unconscious energy absorption could also have roots in childhood/family dynamics. For example, as an empathic or highly sensitive child, I had grown accustomed to attuning to the feelings of others and taking them on as my own. As we get older, we can become more disconnected from our own needs - and fill that space with things like mindless tv watching, overworking, and even take on addictions to alcohol and drugs as a way to self-medicate the burden of being a placeholder for other people's pain.

Bottom line, the lesson is, if it 'aint your shit, you don't have to carry it.

This week, you will learn to reclaim the energy that is yours and let go of the energy and stories that are not yours to carry.

I tap into the magic that spins in all of my cells and I giggle with delight! This magic is out-pictured as my new reality. Ta-Da!

DAILY EXERCISES

MORNING & EVENING | Repeat each of the following elements daily for one week.

MORNING GROUNDING
Start each morning by reading or listening to the 10-minute meditation.

MORNING JOURNALING
In your dedicated journal, take 10 minutes to respond to one or all of the following prompts:

1. Do you identify as a little nurturer? If yes, how did you try to help fix or heal the people in your family (mom, dad, siblings, grandparents, etc.)?

2. Do you feel like you pick up other people's energy? If yes, using the "All The Feels" list, which emotion(s) do you tend to carry for others?

3. How do you feel when you set a boundary or say "no". Is it difficult for you?

4. Self-Devotional Practices
Movement: I will move my body by...
Nourishment: I will feel nourished by...
Your Own: To spark my creativity, I will...

EVENING REFLECTION
At the end of each day, take five minutes to reflect in your journal using one or more of the following prompts:

1. List 1-3 examples of when your mood shifted during the day. Who or what circumstances were connected to that shift?

2. For example, if you were feeling pretty mellow leaving work, but then your cousin texted and suddenly, you felt anxious, try to describe what you felt and any reasons why. This will begin to give you clues to who and what you need to begin setting boundaries with. Great work!

Validate and congratulate yourself before you drift off to sleep.

WEEK IN REVIEW | On the last day of your week, take 5 minutes to reflect in your journal.

WITHOUT JUDGMENT, REVIEW YOUR WEEKLY TRACKER. How many days were you able to implement your self devotional practices? Which practices felt the most balancing? How can you adjust them for the week ahead?

REFLECTING BACK ON THE WEEK, WHAT DID YOU OBSERVE/LEARN FROM THE EXERCISES THIS WEEK? How has this method of returning to your perch helped you? Are you noticing more examples of synchronicity and flow?

SELF-DEVOTION WEEKLY TRACKER

WEEK _____

This is a judgment free zone. Take a moment to record your journey through the daily exercises and devotional practices. Place a check in the box for each exercise you have completed.

Daily Exercises		DAYS OF THE WEEK						
		SU	M	T	W	T	F	S
MORNING GROUNDING	Meditation	○	○	○	○	○	○	○
	Journaling	○	○	○	○	○	○	○
EVENING REFLECTION		○	○	○	○	○	○	○

Self-Devotional Practices

	SU	M	T	W	T	F	S
MOVEMENT _____	○	○	○	○	○	○	○
NOURISHMENT _____	○	○	○	○	○	○	○
YOUR OWN DEVOTION _____	○	○	○	○	○	○	○

Notes

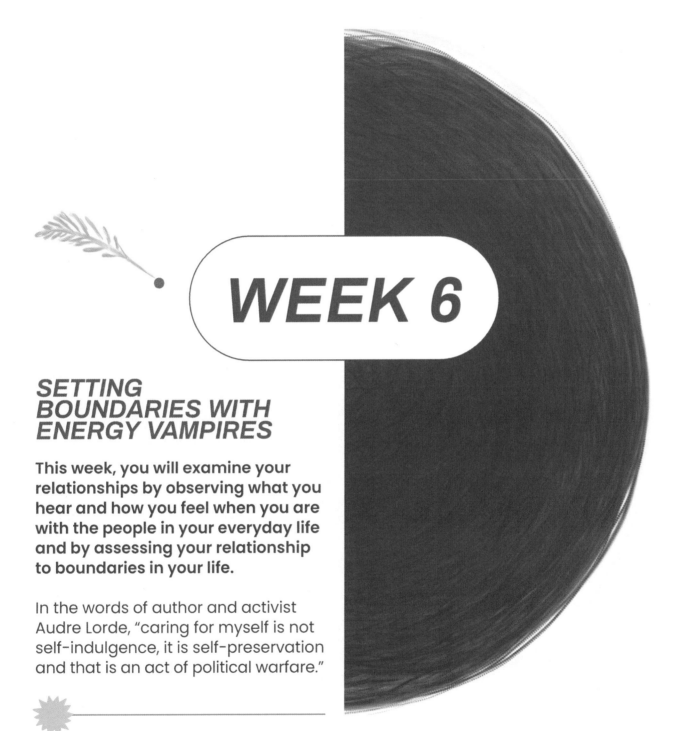

WEEK 6

SETTING BOUNDARIES WITH ENERGY VAMPIRES

This week, you will examine your relationships by observing what you hear and how you feel when you are with the people in your everyday life and by assessing your relationship to boundaries in your life.

In the words of author and activist Audre Lorde, "caring for myself is not self-indulgence, it is self-preservation and that is an act of political warfare."

SETTING BOUNDARIES WITH ENERGY VAMPIRES

The classic vampire archetype pervades myths, fables, as well as pop culture. The story is always the same: this "Creature Of The Night" appears, starving, and some unsuspecting (or suspecting!) individual is inadvertently bitten and drained of his or her blood - their literal lifeforce!

An *energy vampire* isn't much different except, instead of feeding on blood, as the name suggests, the energy vampire feasts on your precious time and energy. They can come in the form of a parent or family member, boss, partner, friend. According to Judith Orloff, MD, there are many different kinds of personality types that fit this description;

- **The Victim:** Someone who wears you out with their "woe is me" stories, whining, and lack of willingness to find solutions.

- **The Passive Aggressive:** Someone who is "angry with a smile" and attacks with verbal jabs that you don't see coming - but make you think, "Ouch! That wasn't very nice."

- **The Rageaholic:** Someone who dumps anger on you, explodes in fits of rage, and spreads toxic energy in their general vicinity.

- **The Narcissist:** Someone who is extremely self-absorbed, manipulative, and fundamentally lacks empathy for others.

Any one of these energy vampires can suck your energy dry if you let them. That is why putting *boundaries* into practice is so important to your mental and emotional health. Unfortunately, if we are accustomed or conditioned from childhood to people please, setting boundaries can feel especially scary. According to melody Beattie, *"boundaries are limits of love. They come from inside of us as honest expressions of who we are. Expect people to test our boundaries. The more they stand to lose, the harder they'll push. They often won't stop pushing until they know we mean what we say"* (Beattie, 2009).

In some communities, such as religious or new age groups, setting boundaries may not be considered the "Christian" or "spiritual" thing to do. In my experience, this couldn't be further from the truth. Whenever we take an action that will preserve our life force and support our mental health, we can rest assured that is what God, the universe, or whatever you believe, intended.

Setting boundaries allows other people to gain clarity on what your needs are and things you are willing to accept. This, in turn, can create a sense of safety for them because it takes the guesswork out of your expectations. In some cases, setting a boundary has improved my relationships, because it created an opportunity for the other person to become aware of their behavior and show up more authentically as themselves.

There is no "wrong way" to set a boundary. For example, with the Victim or Passive Aggressive personality types, limiting the time you spend talking to the person, the amount of energy you invest in offering advice or solutions or simply not answering the phone each time they call, all may qualify as sufficient boundary setting practices.

In contrast, energy vampires such as the Rageaholic, firmer boundaries may be necessary. If a friend, family member or spouse regularly dumps anger at your doorstep, overtime, this can have a toxic effect on your mental, emotional and even physical body. Heart-to-heart conversations, which may include healthy, affirmative statements, such as "I refuse to be spoken to in this way" or "I will not continue this conversation if you insist on screaming at me," also qualify as clear boundaries. Oftentimes, distancing yourself physically, such as hanging up the phone, leaving the room or going no contact, can be appropriate responses, as well.

What all energy vampires have in common is that they have the potential to cause adverse effects to our mental health. So it's important that once you set the boundary, you "hold the fort." This week, you will practice setting boundaries, without guilt or shame, but rather as an act of self-devotion.

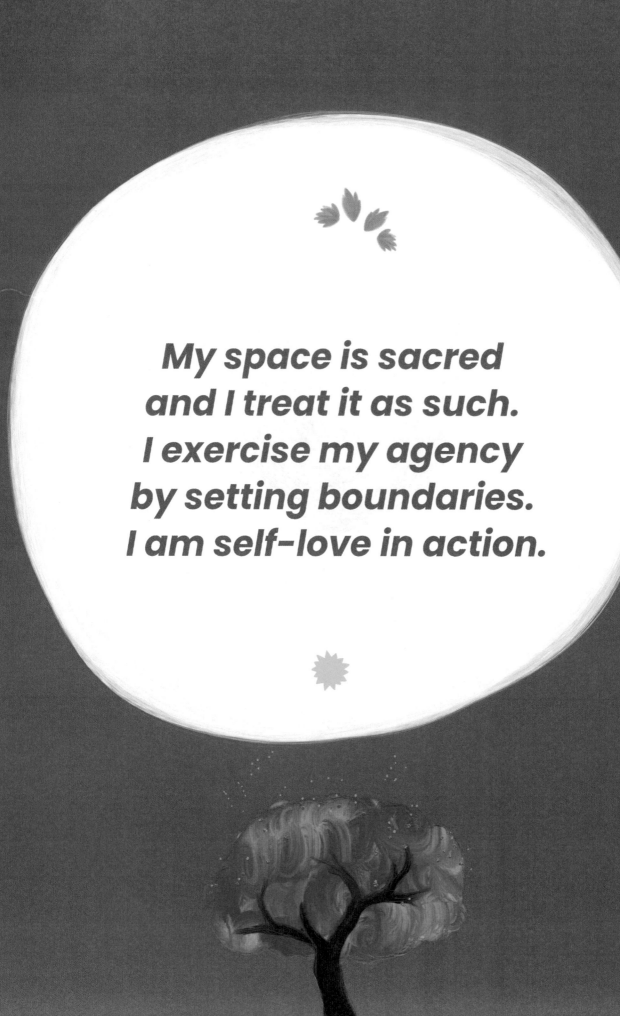

My space is sacred
and I treat it as such.
I exercise my agency
by setting boundaries.
I am self-love in action.

DAILY EXERCISES

MORNING & EVENING Repeat each of the following elements daily for one week.

MORNING GROUNDING
Start each morning by reading or listening to the 10-minute meditation.

MORNING JOURNALING
In your dedicated journal, take 10 minutes to respond to one or all of the following prompts:

1. Which relationships in your life feel reciprocal, fulfilling and life-giving? What is their name and how do you feel when you are around them? (you can use your "All The Feels" list in the appendix for this).

2. Which relationships in your life drain your energy? Do they fit into any of the *energy vampire* categories? If so, what is an example of an appropriate boundary to set with each?

3. What is one action step you can take today to assert your personal power?

4. Self-Devotional Practices
Movement: I will move my body by...
Nourishment: I will feel nourished by...
Your Own: To spark my creativity, I will...

EVENING REFLECTION
At the end of each day, take five minutes to reflect in your journal using one or more of the following prompts:

1. What boundaries do you hold sacred for yourself and with other people in your life? When you set a boundary, are they honored by the people around you? Are you able to maintain the boundaries you have set? If Yes, how?

2. Thinking about the people you spent time with today (this could be in person or virtual), with whom did you feel your best? With whom did you feel drained or different?

3. Did you have to implement a boundary today? If yes, what was it and how did you feel about naming it?

Validate and congratulate yourself before you drift off to sleep.

WEEK IN REVIEW On the last day of your week, take 5 minutes to reflect in your journal.

WITHOUT JUDGMENT, REVIEW YOUR WEEKLY TRACKER. How many days were you able to implement your self devotional practices? Which practices felt the most balancing? How can you adjust them for the week ahead?

REFLECTING BACK ON THE WEEK, WHAT DID YOU OBSERVE/LEARN FROM THE EXERCISES THIS WEEK? How has this method of returning to your perch helped you? Are you noticing more examples of synchronicity and flow?

SELF-DEVOTION WEEKLY TRACKER

WEEK _____

This is a judgment free zone. Take a moment to record your journey through the daily exercises and devotional practices. Place a check in the box for each exercise you have completed.

Daily Exercises		DAYS OF THE WEEK						
		SU	M	T	W	T	F	S
MORNING GROUNDING								
Meditation		○	○	○	○	○	○	○
Journaling		○	○	○	○	○	○	○
EVENING REFLECTION		○	○	○	○	○	○	○

Self-Devotional Practices

	SU	M	T	W	T	F	S
MOVEMENT _____	○	○	○	○	○	○	○
NOURISHMENT _____	○	○	○	○	○	○	○
YOUR OWN DEVOTION _____	○	○	○	○	○	○	○

Notes

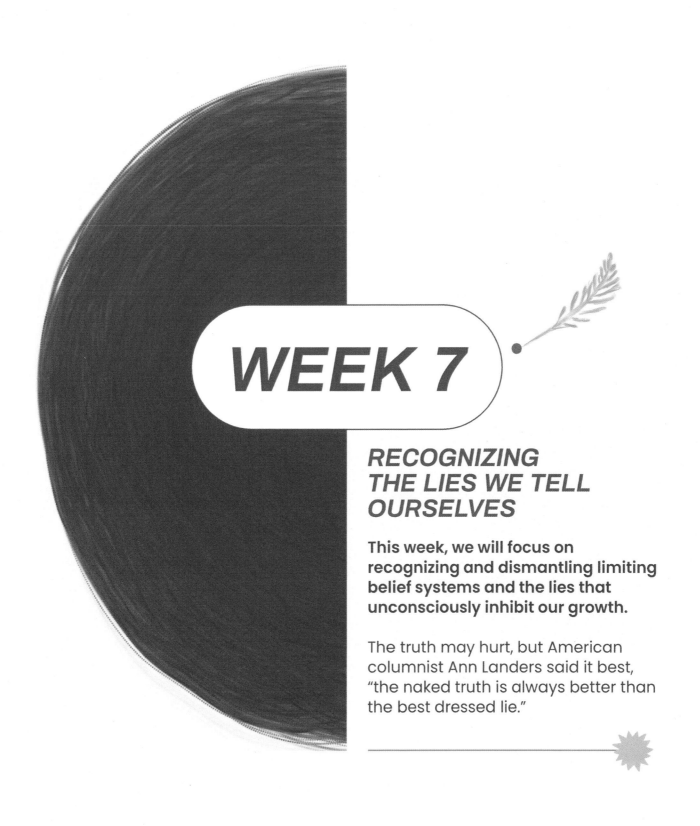

WEEK 7

RECOGNIZING THE LIES WE TELL OURSELVES

This week, we will focus on recognizing and dismantling limiting belief systems and the lies that unconsciously inhibit our growth.

The truth may hurt, but American columnist Ann Landers said it best, "the naked truth is always better than the best dressed lie."

RECOGNIZING THE LIES WE TELL OURSELVES

Lies are formed when someone projects their ideas or values onto you and you believe it, or internalize a story (that isn't true) to protect yourself. These limiting and debilitating belief systems can be born out of fear, survival and trauma. They inform our reality completely and they operate secretly in the subconscious, perpetuating patterns, oftentimes under the radar of our awareness. Eventually, they become the "lies" we tell ourselves.

The good news is that there is a signal that is constantly broadcasting. This signal is called *truth*. It is who you are at your core, the blueprint you arrived with upon entering this current reality on Earth. The problem is lies and false projections about ourselves act like debris that distorts the signal, temporarily drowning out the subtle yet steady pulsing of your truth.

Some examples include:

- "I am worthless."
- "I always mess up."
- "I can't do it."
- "I am unlovable."
- "Life is hard."
- "I am not enough."
- "I will always be alone."
- "I am only worthy if someone chooses me for a mate."

A poignant and powerful scripture in the Bible states: "Every kingdom divided against itself is brought to desolation, and every city or house divided against itself will not stand" (Matthew 12:22). Within the context of this week, we seek to root out the lies tucked away in our psyche that threaten to divide us and separate us from our own unique vibration, our truth, our authentic self - our happiness. True integrity requires that we live in alignment with our soul's truth.

The body naturally pushes out poison. When we raise your vibration by anchoring more to truth (your natural vibration), lies and outdated belief systems will begin to reveal themselves.

This week, you will begin to notice the "lies" in your mind and reframe them. This may seem daunting, but here is the good news. Lies begin to dissolve the movement we call them out.

**My mind is a den
of peace as I center
down into the one truth:
I am love – perfect,
whole and complete.**

DAILY EXERCISES

MORNING & EVENING | Repeat each of the following elements daily for one week.

MORNING GROUNDING
Start each morning by reading or listening to the 10-minute meditation.

MORNING JOURNALING
In your dedicated journal, take 10 minutes to respond to one or all of the following prompts:

1. During the meditation, what "lies" did you notice emerge? Was there one that stood out to you, specifically?

2. Whose voice(s) are behind these lies? Think about the people closest to you (friends, family, colleagues, community, etc.). Are you able to identify the origin(s)?

3. Self-Devotional Practices
Movement: I will move my body by...
Nourishment: I will feel nourished by...
Your Own: To spark my creativity, I will...

EVENING REFLECTION
At the end of each day, take five minutes to reflect in your journal using one or more of the following prompts:

Are you able to recall a moment in your day when the mind weaved a story or created commentary on any given subject, person or circumstance? Jot down a few quick notes in your journal about your observations.

Validate and congratulate yourself before you drift off to sleep.

WEEK IN REVIEW | On the last day of your week, take 5 minutes to reflect in your journal.

WITHOUT JUDGMENT, REVIEW YOUR WEEKLY TRACKER. How many days were you able to implement your self devotional practices? Which practices felt the most balancing? How can you adjust them for the week ahead?

REFLECTING BACK ON THE WEEK, WHAT DID YOU OBSERVE/LEARN FROM THE EXERCISES THIS WEEK? How has this method of returning to your perch helped you? Are you noticing more examples of synchronicity and flow?

SELF-DEVOTION WEEKLY TRACKER

WEEK _____

This is a judgment free zone. Take a moment to record your journey through the daily exercises and devotional practices. Place a check in the box for each exercise you have completed.

Daily Exercises

DAYS OF THE WEEK

	SU	M	T	W	T	F	S
MORNING GROUNDING							
Meditation	○	○	○	○	○	○	○
Journaling	○	○	○	○	○	○	○
EVENING REFLECTION	○	○	○	○	○	○	○

Self-Devotional Practices

	SU	M	T	W	T	F	S
MOVEMENT _____	○	○	○	○	○	○	○
NOURISHMENT _____	○	○	○	○	○	○	○
YOUR OWN DEVOTION _____	○	○	○	○	○	○	○

Notes

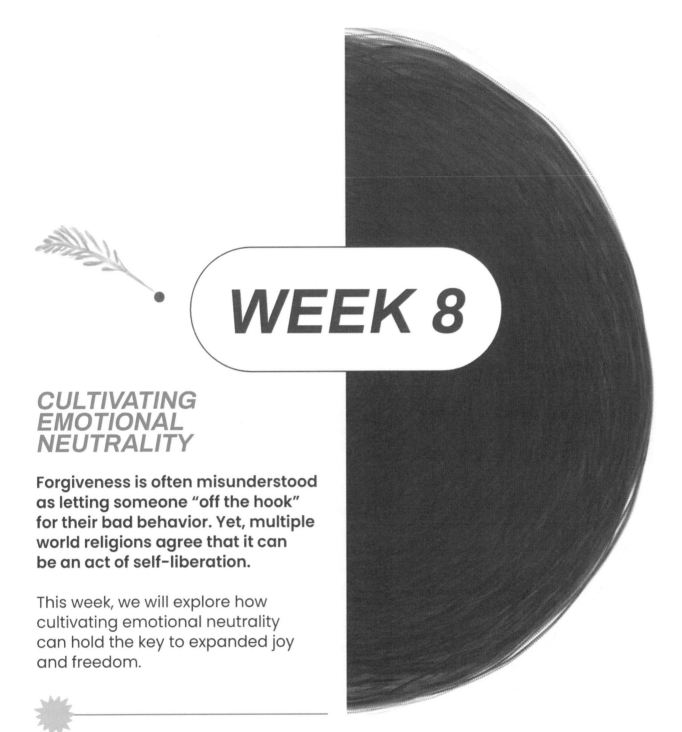

WEEK 8

CULTIVATING EMOTIONAL NEUTRALITY

Forgiveness is often misunderstood as letting someone "off the hook" for their bad behavior. Yet, multiple world religions agree that it can be an act of self-liberation.

This week, we will explore how cultivating emotional neutrality can hold the key to expanded joy and freedom.

CULTIVATING EMOTIONAL NEUTRALITY

What comes to mind when you consider the word neutrality? Boredom? Calm? Switzerland? To be neutral is to be "free of charge". This is a powerful state of being. As we continue to learn the fine art of raising and changing our vibration, we will come to see neutrality as a resting place: our natural state and our own, authentic vibration.

What would it be like to be "free of charge"? This week, we will explore this non-reactive state, this place of "unbotherability'. Being neutral doesn't mean we don't care - it simply means we are impervious to the energy of those around us. That no matter the insanity or chaos we may find ourselves in, we are able to hold our own unique vibration.

In order to do this we must be aware of our triggers. When we feel "triggered", we are responding to outside stimuli touching one of our (sometimes hidden) wounds. Isn't it interesting that we tend to attract those people and situations that know how to push our buttons, in just the right way?

Another way of cultivating neutrality is to become aware of the resentments we are harboring and those folks we are still holding hostage. You know, the ones that have wronged us, or betrayed us. In reality, we imprison ourselves when we continue to hold on to the trauma and wounds of the past. **We aren't letting someone else off the hook when we forgive, we are unlocking our own cages, setting ourselves free and creating more precious space. Space to live, love and create, without limit.**

During your daily practice, do a quick body scan and notice if there is any "charge" present. It could be left over anger at a person or situation from last week's practice. Notice any emotions that come or go as you release down the *grounding cord* and through your feet. Imagine yourself as a *"body of glass."* Notice any spots or anything that clouds this glass.

*I forgive myself and
begin again knowing
that the renewal
of my mind is only
a breath, a meditation,
a song away...*

DAILY EXERCISES

MORNING & EVENING
Repeat each of the following elements daily for one week.

MORNING GROUNDING
Start each morning by reading or listening to the 10-minute meditation.

MORNING JOURNALING
In your dedicated journal, take 10 minutes to respond to one or all of the following prompts:

1. What was the first thing that came to mind when you considered "neutrality" as a state of being?

2. What are examples of neutrality? Look at nature, your environment, your workplace, and the personalities of the people you know.

3. Were you able to see yourself as a body of glass? Did you see any spots or blemishes?

4. Self-Devotional Practices
Movement: I will move my body by...
Nourishment: I will feel nourished by...
Your Own: To spark my creativity, I will...

EVENING REFLECTION
At the end of each day, take five minutes to reflect in your journal using one or more of the following prompts:

1. Each night, take notice of when people "pushed your buttons" throughout the day.

2. What words describe the way you felt during these moments? Using the "All The Feels," list the emotions or "pet-peeves" that emerge.

3. Observe from a place of curiosity, like you are opening a book for the first time. Write your observations in a journal.

Validate and congratulate yourself before you drift off to sleep.

WEEK IN REVIEW
On the last day of your week, take 5 minutes to reflect in your journal.

WITHOUT JUDGMENT, REVIEW YOUR WEEKLY TRACKER. How many days were you able to implement your self devotional practices? Which practices felt the most balancing? How can you adjust them for the week ahead?

REFLECTING BACK ON THE WEEK, WHAT DID YOU OBSERVE/LEARN FROM THE EXERCISES THIS WEEK? How has this method of returning to your perch helped you? Are you noticing more examples of synchronicity and flow?

SELF-DEVOTION WEEKLY TRACKER

WEEK _____

This is a judgment free zone. Take a moment to record your journey through the daily exercises and devotional practices. Place a check in the box for each exercise you have completed.

Daily Exercises		DAYS OF THE WEEK						
		SU	M	T	W	T	F	S
MORNING GROUNDING								
Meditation		○	○	○	○	○	○	○
Journaling		○	○	○	○	○	○	○
EVENING REFLECTION		○	○	○	○	○	○	○

Self-Devotional Practices

	SU	M	T	W	T	F	S
MOVEMENT _____	○	○	○	○	○	○	○
NOURISHMENT _____	○	○	○	○	○	○	○
YOUR OWN DEVOTION _____	○	○	○	○	○	○	○

Notes

MODULE 2 IN REVIEW

CONGRATULATIONS ON COMPLETING MODULE TWO! TAKE A MOMENT TO REFLECT ON YOUR JOURNEY SO FAR IN YOUR JOURNAL.

Without judgment, looking across your weekly tracker, how many days were you able to implement your self-devotional practices this month? What did you learn from adding these practices into your daily life?

Reflecting back on the past month, what are your top learnings from this module? How did your experience during this module differ from your experience in Module One? How is it the same?

To close out the month, what are you most proud of and how can you celebrate all that you have accomplished thus far?

INTEGRATING THE COSMOS

WELCOME TO MODULE THREE

We are in the home stretch! Take a moment to congratulate yourself on a job well done! In this final module, we will be integrating all of the tools and practices you've been learning for the past two months. We begin by "upgrading" our "terms" and signing a brand new contract with ourselves. Then, we will experience firsthand some of the benefits of empowerment as a state of being, including increased creativity, inspiration and an innate sense of safety. Finally, we will conclude our journey by exploring "power" - our relationship to it, how it's been misused and most importantly, how we can experience *sustainable* authentic empowerment by anchoring into the "I Am" presence.

WEEK 9	**Upgrading Your "Terms Of Service"**
WEEK 10	**Awakening To Your Creative Power**
WEEK 11	**Finding Safety In Change**
WEEK 12	**The "I Am" Presence**

Daily Exercises

This module will focus on establishing a 35-minute grounding practice.

Building on the practices established in Modules One and Two, the final four weeks focus on adding 5 additional minutes to your meditation practice. Each morning, you will complete this 15-minute meditation, morning and evening journaling prompts, as well as a checklist to track your progress.

I encourage you to set aside 35 minutes each day, 30 minutes in the morning to meditate and journal, and 5 minutes for reflection in the evening to gain the most benefit from the practice.

15 MINUTE MEDITATION

You can utilize this recording to guide you in your grounding practice.

🎧 LISTEN HERE

Take a seat and let's begin!

If comfortable or appropriate, close your eyes, or simply turn your gaze downwards.

In your mind's eye, trace a mental circle around yourself, as if you were able to visualize where your energetic field begins and ends. Experiment with arm's length, then tracing the circle farther out. Notice what feels safest for you. **This is your *space* - your energetic boundary.**

Bring your attention to the bottoms of the feet. Begin to sense the connection between your feet and the earth. Then, in your mind's eye, draw a line of energy from the bottoms of your feet into the center of the earth. **This is a fantastic opportunity to give yourself permission to activate the imagination.**

Sense this line of energy moving from the bottom of the feet, through the floorboards, the layers of rock and sediment underneath you, until it reaches the core of the planet. Once you are able to experience this connection, allow the line of energy to expand, perhaps forming into sturdy roots.

Allow the imagery to emerge in your mind's eye, naturally. Perhaps, another image comes to mind: a waterfall or rays of light. As your feet begin to ground into the Earth, allow any remaining tension, stress or rigidity to release down through the grounding roots at the base of the feet.

Stay here, breathing and releasing, until you begin to feel steady, calm and centered.

Then, bring your attention to the base of the spine, or the point of connection between your body and the seat of your chair. Then, in your mind's eye, draw a line of energy from your seat into the center of the earth. When you sense this connection, watch the line of energy expand into a grounding cord, widening to the width of your chair. Perhaps, you can visualize yourself sitting on a Redwood tree stump, or allow any other imagery that resonates with you to naturally emerge.

Postulate a chair or seat in the center of the mind. **Bring your attention to this space, this room behind your eyes and then allow it to rest in this chair or seat. This is your "perch".**

Begin to notice this shift in perspective, almost as if you are able to simply observe your emotions, thoughts and feelings from this viewpoint. Then, ground the mind by visualizing a line of energy extending from the center of the mind into the center of the planet. Allow the line of energy to expand and release any tension, stress or racing thoughts down through the mind and into the center of the earth. Continue to breathe.

In this module, we are going to incorporate *cosmic energy* to create a sense of balance and cohesion with the earth/grounding energy we've been working with.

Begin by imagining you are able to pull in fresh earth energy through the feet. Visualize this energy traveling up through the legs, curving at the pelvis, into the base of the spine and allow it to trickle down the grounding cord and into the earth. Breathe into this experience for a few moments and feel the body ground.

Next, bring your attention to the crown of your head. Imagine your crown opening (similar to when you give yourself a golden sun) and postulate a clear, neutral point in the sky (no planets or stars, just a nice open space). Then, visualize this (neutral) cosmic energy pouring into your crown and traveling down your spine and down your grounding cord.

Now, allow some of that cosmic energy to mix with the earth energy in the base of your spine. I like to work with 90% cosmic and 10% Earth. Feel free to experiment! Maybe you would like to try 80% earth and 20% cosmic. Then, bring this mixture up through the front of the body.

Breathe deeply and relax as you experience this earth and cosmic mix move through your sacrum, solar plexus, heart, throat, into the center of your head (perch) and down your arms. Then, let this mix fountain out the crown of the head and around the body, cleansing your entire field.

Stay here as long as you like, allowing this mix of earth and cosmic energy to cleanse your field. As you feel the feelings that accompany this beautiful process of validating yourself, you can close this practice with a golden sun.

Sense this golden sun above your head and allow it to fill with golden light. As it fills, begin to watch as it overflows and fills you up like a cup, into the feet, ankles, the legs. Going at your own pace, allow the golden sun to move into your seat and down the grounding cord, the solar plexus, the heart, the shoulders.

Breathe as you receive, allowing yourself to receive fully. Allow the golden sun to fill in the places and spaces where you let go of something and/or released energy. When you feel completely full of the golden sun, begin to bring slight movements to the body, validating yourself for sitting in the stillness, for this amount of time, increasing your practice over the weeks to now, this full 15 minute practice.

As a bonus practice, we will add one more step. First, notice yourself in this embodied state, this state of self-exaltation. What color are you seeing? What is a color that represents this embodied state? Notice its texture, notice if it has a sparkle. This isn't "prescriptive" color and it may change from day to day. This is a color that encapsulates you, in this present moment.

When you see this color, allow it to rest on your crown, or you can wrap it around yourself like a blanket. This is your power color, a color that cultivates a sense of empowerment, balance, safety.

If at any point throughout your day, you begin to feel dysregulated or you need a boost, bring this color to your mind, to your crown or to your heart and it will help bring you back to this balanced state.

Take a few more breaths. The exercise is complete. You are connected!

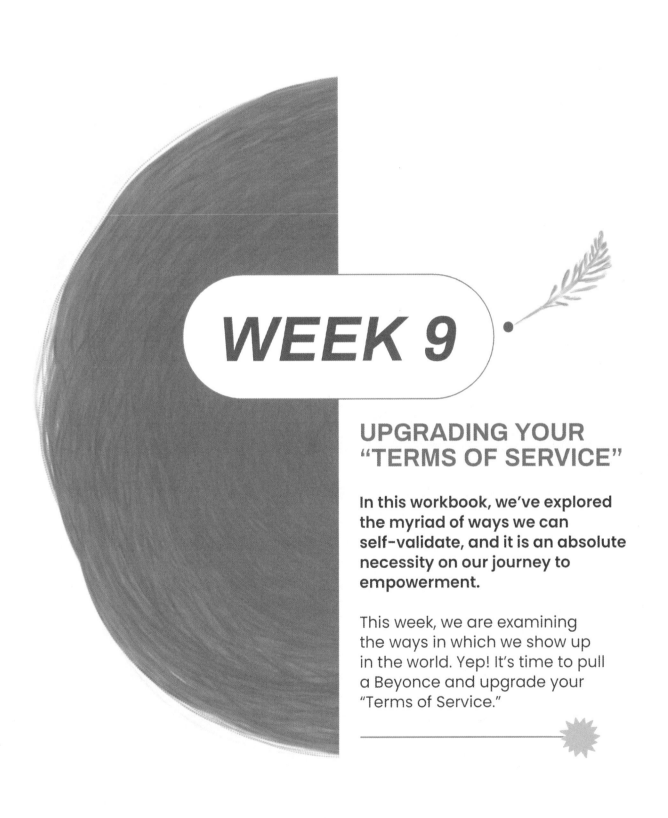

WEEK 9

UPGRADING YOUR "TERMS OF SERVICE"

In this workbook, we've explored the myriad of ways we can self-validate, and it is an absolute necessity on our journey to empowerment.

This week, we are examining the ways in which we show up in the world. Yep! It's time to pull a Beyonce and upgrade your "Terms of Service."

UPGRADING YOUR "TERMS OF SERVICE"

You may have already begun to notice the ripples of change in your daily life - perhaps your spouse, family, co-workers or friends are subtly (or not so subtly) noting how you have "changed" or that you "seem different." If the earth is beginning to feel like it's shifting under your feet, no need to hit the panic button.

The external world - conditions, circumstances and our relationships - are but an outpicturing of our internal world. Here is one of my favorite examples: when I was living in NYC back in 2005, I would marvel at the folks who could get signal underground on the subway. when I would ask, they would inevitably say they have "Verizon." Meanwhile, I had T-Mobile, so at that time, getting a signal underground was virtually impossible.

Our thoughts, emotions and intentions operate in a similar way. **The more we release density - pain, resentment, shame, worry and fear - the lighter we become.** Our signal becomes clearer. Subsequently, we are more "connected" - our intentions and desires manifest more quickly because our signal is strong enough to cut through the density of physical reality.

So, instead of just absent-mindedly clicking "agree" when our smartphone sends us that lengthy "Terms of Service" agreement, we are taking the time to read through and discern if the "service agreements" we had in the past, are indeed still working for us.

As a result, we have "changed our space" and raised our vibration. So, we need to continue to address, examine and update the agreements we have with the people and situations in our lives. In your daily practice, from your perch, inquire who you have contracts with that need to be adjusted or updated. One by one, notice who emerges. See them in their highest version and imagine they are sitting across from you, but outside of your space. Review the contract. See yourself making adjustments, and/or voiding the contract completely if it is no longer serving you. When complete, give each person a golden rose and watch them walk away. Fill up with a golden sun.

*I hold
the highest
vision for
my life each
and every day.*

DAILY EXERCISES

MORNING & EVENING
Repeat each of the following elements daily for one week.

MORNING GROUNDING
Start each morning by reading or listening to the 15-minute meditation.

MORNING JOURNALING
In your dedicated journal, take 10 minutes to respond to one or all of the following prompts:

1. Who would you consider your "contracts" to be with? Write about each person and the nature of the contract you feel you hold with them.

- State the behaviors, belief systems and patterning from which you are breaking your vow with.

- State what you are now in service to (love, peace and happiness, filling your own well before you attempt to support others, etc.).

2. Were you surprised at the "conditions" and "terms" you discovered? Write about any "aha" moments.

3. Self-Devotional Practices
Movement: I will move my body by...
Nourishment: I will feel nourished by...
Your Own: To spark my creativity, I will...

EVENING REFLECTION
At the end of each day, take five minutes to reflect in your journal using one or more of the following prompts:

Pay close attention to your interactions with those whom you've updated your "terms" with. Each night review (with *amusement*) your different interactions. Use the "All The Feels" list to help you.

1. Name the person and note any patterns. For example, with them did you feel like healing, fixing, carrying the load, or absorbing energy?

2. Did you notice anything else?

3. Knowing this, what could you change for the next time you see them?

Validate and congratulate yourself before you drift off to sleep.

WEEK IN REVIEW
On the last day of your week, take 5 minutes to reflect in your journal.

WITHOUT JUDGMENT, REVIEW YOUR WEEKLY TRACKER. How many days were you able to implement your self devotional practices? Which practices felt the most balancing? How can you adjust them for the week ahead?

REFLECTING BACK ON THE WEEK, WHAT DID YOU OBSERVE/LEARN FROM THE EXERCISES THIS WEEK? How has this method of returning to your perch helped you? Are you noticing more examples of synchronicity and flow?

SELF-DEVOTION WEEKLY TRACKER

WEEK _____

This is a judgment free zone. Take a moment to record your journey through the daily exercises and devotional practices. Place a check in the box for each exercise you have completed.

Daily Exercises

DAYS OF THE WEEK

Daily Exercises	SU	M	T	W	T	F	S
MORNING GROUNDING							
Meditation	○	○	○	○	○	○	○
Journaling	○	○	○	○	○	○	○
EVENING REFLECTION	○	○	○	○	○	○	○

Self-Devotional Practices

	SU	M	T	W	T	F	S
MOVEMENT _____	○	○	○	○	○	○	○
NOURISHMENT _____	○	○	○	○	○	○	○
YOUR OWN DEVOTION _____	○	○	○	○	○	○	○

Notes

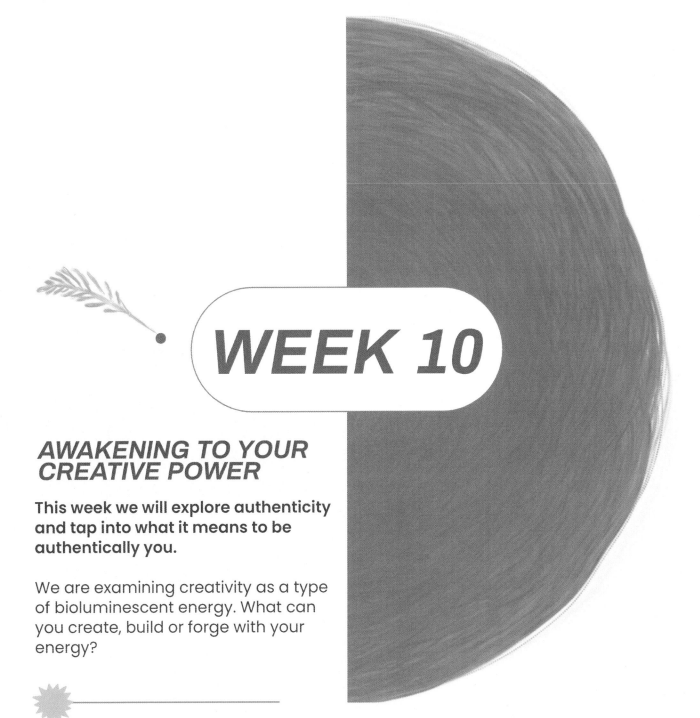

WEEK 10

AWAKENING TO YOUR CREATIVE POWER

This week we will explore authenticity and tap into what it means to be authentically you.

We are examining creativity as a type of bioluminescent energy. What can you create, build or forge with your energy?

AWAKENING TO YOUR CREATIVE POWER

A great teacher once stated that when we try to emulate others, it's like committing a character assassination on ourselves. In a society that encourages us to be everyone except ourselves, it can be a challenge to step into one's authenticity. But, it is tantamount to our growth and wellness as human beings. Why? Because when we step into alignment with our own authenticity, then opportunities and success unfold organically and "authentically".

Serendipity and synchronicity take hold. Opportunities and relationships show up as if timed by forces in the unseen. The truth is, we are all interconnected. But at the same time, we are unique expressions of the one. **What does it mean to be authentic to you?**

This "real you" is not based on your color, creed, upbringing, belief systems or even your bank account balance, career level or your current mood. These are all circumstantial and transitory. Your true self is pristine and untarnished - similar to an eternal blue sky. The circumstantial and the transitory are the "clouds" that pass by. Visible and seemingly "real" but not *who* you are.

Throughout this program, we have spent time cultivating tools to regulate our emotions and vehicles of expression. This week it is all about examining creativity as a type of bioluminescent energy. Our culture tends to cage creativity, doling it out for only some to utilize. Creativity is constantly emanating, it just needs a vessel to express through.

It's time to awaken the true essence of your being and unleash your creative power. It is likely stronger than you may think!

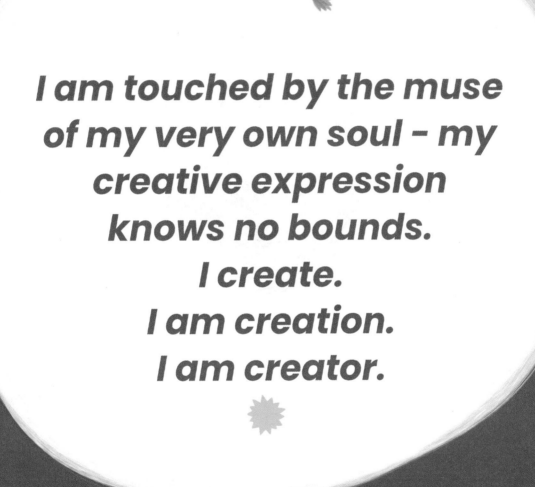

I am touched by the muse
of my very own soul – my
creative expression
knows no bounds.
I create.
I am creation.
I am creator.

DAILY EXERCISES

MORNING & EVENING | Repeat each of the following elements daily for one week.

MORNING GROUNDING
Start each morning by reading or listening to the 15-minute meditation.

MORNING JOURNALING
In your dedicated journal, take 10 minutes to respond to one or all of the following prompts:

1. Did you receive messages, opinions or directives in your life that led you to believe that you couldn't "make a living" as a creative person or that it wasn't the "practical" thing to do?

2. Did you have a childhood dream of doing something creative when you grew up? What's one step you can take today to tap into or recover your creative self?

3. Self-Devotional Practices
Movement: I will move my body by...
Nourishment: I will feel nourished by...
Your Own: To spark my creativity, I will...

EVENING REFLECTION
At the end of each day, take five minutes to reflect in your journal using one or more of the following prompts:

1. What did you do to validate yourself today? As you reflect on your day, take note of your "wins".

2. Notice when you may have minimized or overlooked an accomplishment. (This may show up as calling it a "small victory"). Create a practice of writing down at least two wins each day.

Congratulate yourself before you drift off to sleep.

WEEK IN REVIEW | On the last day of your week, take 5 minutes to reflect in your journal.

WITHOUT JUDGMENT, REVIEW YOUR WEEKLY TRACKER. How many days were you able to implement your self devotional practices? Which practices felt the most balancing? How can you adjust them for the week ahead?

REFLECTING BACK ON THE WEEK, WHAT DID YOU OBSERVE/LEARN FROM THE EXERCISES THIS WEEK? How has this method of returning to your perch helped you? Are you noticing more examples of synchronicity and flow?

SELF-DEVOTION WEEKLY TRACKER

WEEK _____

This is a judgment free zone. Take a moment to record your journey through the daily exercises and devotional practices. Place a check in the box for each exercise you have completed.

Daily Exercises

DAYS OF THE WEEK

	SU	M	T	W	T	F	S
MORNING GROUNDING							
Meditation	○	○	○	○	○	○	○
Journaling	○	○	○	○	○	○	○
EVENING REFLECTION	○	○	○	○	○	○	○

Self-Devotional Practices

	SU	M	T	W	T	F	S
MOVEMENT _____	○	○	○	○	○	○	○
NOURISHMENT _____	○	○	○	○	○	○	○
YOUR OWN DEVOTION _____	○	○	○	○	○	○	○

Notes

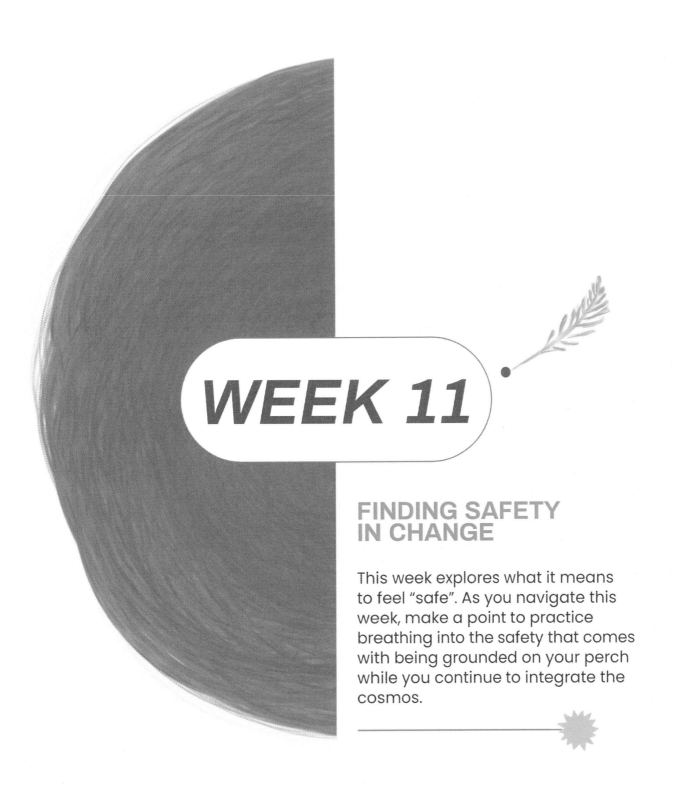

WEEK 11

FINDING SAFETY IN CHANGE

This week explores what it means to feel "safe". As you navigate this week, make a point to practice breathing into the safety that comes with being grounded on your perch while you continue to integrate the cosmos.

FINDING SAFETY IN CHANGE

How do you find safety in a world where change is the only constant? How do you avoid being carried like a leaf on the wind, every time something unexpected happens? Perhaps the most secure place you can find safety is within.

"Finding Safety In Change" is one of the last weeks because it is perhaps the most important. **This workbook is designed to foster a stronger sense of self, to assist you in finding your space, increase your trust in yourself, others and the universe, and to provide you with a solid spiritual practice that supports you.**

In the words of Robert Neimeyer, "in a world of impermanence, we humans are wired for attachment. It is how we negotiate that tension that shapes who we become (Dixit, 2010). So, if you continue to glean your peace of mind and a sense of safety from objects, people, places and things, you are at the mercy of an ever-changing world. You risk intensifying the emotional and spiritual rollercoaster caused by the uncertainty inherent in human life.

There is a reason why people may feel safe in their church, home, a 12-Step meeting, a support group that meets every Tuesday night, or even a monthly book club. These places and spaces can act as anchors or benchmarks. Like the batman cartoon used to say, "same bat time, same bat place." Ritual and community, fused with some type of "food" for thought or the soul, has the potential to create the continuity and stability that steadies our minds and hearts.

More specifically, over the past few months, you have dedicated time and energy to discovering and curating self-devotional practices as a way to resource yourself. By now, you may notice a pattern. What are the practices, tools and behaviors that you find provide the most *object constancy* and an overall sense of calm and well-being?

Then, if you were to take a look at your checklist, how many of those things are reliable and unconditional? In other words, how many of those things don't "move"? Examples may be your grounding practice, movement practice, creative expression or even a friend, family member or spouse you can rely on.

If you are seeking safety, the answer may lie in your commitment to the practices that facilitate, maintain and sustain that deep, abiding connection to that steady, guiding and protective presence within. This week, you will deepen your ability to seek and discover an unchanging safety that lies within.

I seek and discover magic around every corner, in every area of my life. I am the heroine of my own fantastical journey!

DAILY EXERCISES

MORNING & EVENING | Repeat each of the following elements daily for one week.

MORNING GROUNDING
Start each morning by reading or listening to the 15-minute meditation.

MORNING JOURNALING
In your dedicated journal, take 5 minutes to respond to one or all of the following prompts:

1. What is your "MO" when you feel scared or unsafe? Do you run, hide, freeze, fight? List a few of your reactions, vices, etc.

2. Draw a circle on a page of your journal. Inside of your circle, list the go-to self-devotional practices that help you feel the most grounded and/or create the most object constancy. Then, add in your most trusted friends, family or community members. These are your core resources that help you cultivate a sense of safety. They are reliable and unconditional. Refer to this circle any time you feel unsafe, dysregulated or contracted.

3. Self-Devotional Practices
Movement: I will move my body by...
Nourishment: I will feel nourished by...
Your Own: To spark my creativity, I will...

EVENING REFLECTION
At the end of each day, take five minutes to reflect in your journal using one or more of the following prompts:

1. Note the moments in your day when you felt unsafe or fearful and note why. Pay close attention to your body (tugs or butterflies in the tummy, shooting pains, cramps or any type of contraction). Also, note the moments you felt safe or cultivated a sense of safety for yourself.

2. Before drifting off to sleep, remember a time when you felt completely loved and/or celebrated. Close your eyes and see if you can imagine this feeling as a color. Begin to magnify the color watching it increase in size and intensity. As you breathe in/out, begin to notice the color enveloping you and feel the sensation of unconditional love and forgiveness wash over you.

Whenever you are ready, validate and congratulate yourself before you drift off to sleep.

WEEK IN REVIEW | On the last day of your week, take 5 minutes to reflect in your journal.

WITHOUT JUDGMENT, REVIEW YOUR WEEKLY TRACKER. How many days were you able to implement your self devotional practices? Which practices felt the most balancing? How can you adjust them for the week ahead?

REFLECTING BACK ON THE WEEK, WHAT DID YOU OBSERVE/LEARN FROM THE EXERCISES THIS WEEK? How has this method of returning to your perch helped you? Are you noticing more examples of synchronicity and flow?

SELF-DEVOTION WEEKLY TRACKER

WEEK _____

This is a judgment free zone. Take a moment to record your journey through the daily exercises and devotional practices. Place a check in the box for each exercise you have completed.

Daily Exercises

DAYS OF THE WEEK

	SU	M	T	W	T	F	S
MORNING GROUNDING							
Meditation	○	○	○	○	○	○	○
Journaling	○	○	○	○	○	○	○
EVENING REFLECTION	○	○	○	○	○	○	○

Self-Devotional Practices

	SU	M	T	W	T	F	S
MOVEMENT _____	○	○	○	○	○	○	○
NOURISHMENT _____	○	○	○	○	○	○	○
YOUR OWN DEVOTION _____	○	○	○	○	○	○	○

Notes

WEEK 12

THE "I AM" PRESENCE

In the final week, we will seal your practice. You may have noticed you are cultivating a magnetic like quality in yourself.

This is your "I AM" presence.

THE "I AM" PRESENCE

THEME OF THE WEEK

What is the difference between authentic power and pseudo-power? How do you know which one you are looking at? Here is a clue: pseudo-power is power that is exacted over others by others. **Authentic power radiates from within.** We see examples of the former in government. We elect "officials" and then we place them into positions of power. Some of these folks are not empowered individuals. They derive a sense of power from exerting control over the masses. This is pseudo power.

More often than not, we give away our power. To our credit, we are programmed that way. We are raised to fear and to obey without question those who are in power. We go to school and learn quickly how to fall in line with trends of the moment, which plants the seed for "group think." We give our peers the power to pressure us into questionable or dangerous behavior. We fall in love and give away our power to our significant other, oftentimes with the secret or unconscious desire for the other to fix us, fill us or heal us.

Sometimes we even suppress our power to make others feel more comfortable. We may have learned at an early age that to shine and to place our brilliance on display like peacock feathers caused us to be bullied, judged or cut down in some way. So, we dim our light to be liked, accepted, to not rock the boat. This is a subtle form of control and serves no one, especially not ourselves.

But, to be empowered is to have a direct line to one's own inner divinity, soul, "I AM" presence and all of the other words for that ineffable presence that lies within. Most of us walk around completely oblivious to our inner power or have difficulty accessing it. When we receive a "Hello!" - from ourselves or another - we are opening and aligning with this "I AM" presence. In essence, we are remembering *who* and *whose* we really are. This week will help us to tap into the inner well of our hidden power.

*I leave the past as it is
and give thanks for it
because it led me to now -
where all of my
dreams are coming true.*

DAILY EXERCISES

MORNING & EVENING Repeat each of the following elements daily for one week.

MORNING GROUNDING
Start each morning by reading or listening to the 15-minute meditation.

MORNING JOURNALING
In your dedicated journal, take 5 minutes to respond to one or all of the following prompts:

1. What is your first memory/experience of your power? Name 3 people you feel stand in their power. Who are the most empowered people you know?

2. During your daily meditation, did you see anyone's face flash in your mind as the sun drew your power back? Note any feelings, sensations or images ormemories that emerged during your practice.

3. Self-Devotional Practices
Movement: I will move my body by...
Nourishment: I will feel nourished by...
Your Own: To spark my creativity, I will...

EVENING REFLECTION
At the end of each day, take five minutes to reflect in your journal using one or more of the following prompts:

1. Throughout the week, notice the ways that power shows up in your life.

- Take note of moments when you feel that someone is trying to overpower you or vice versa.

- Notice moments when you assert your power in constructive and positive ways, such as making a choice, setting a boundary or saying "no".

- Notice when you give your power away. Observe with compassion and then note your discoveries in your journal.

2. Before going to sleep, think of anyone you have encountered throughout the day that you let take your power, close your eyes and visualize them giving you your energy/power back with a golden sun.

Validate and congratulate yourself before you drift off to sleep.

WEEK IN REVIEW On the last day of your week, take 5 minutes to reflect in your journal.

WITHOUT JUDGMENT, REVIEW YOUR WEEKLY TRACKER. How many days were you able to implement your self devotional practices? Which practices felt the most balancing? How can you adjust them for the week ahead?

REFLECTING BACK ON THE WEEK, WHAT DID YOU OBSERVE/LEARN FROM THE EXERCISES THIS WEEK? How has this method of returning to your perch helped you? Are you noticing more examples of synchronicity and flow?

SELF-DEVOTION WEEKLY TRACKER

WEEK _____

This is a judgment free zone. Take a moment to record your journey through the daily exercises and devotional practices. Place a check in the box for each exercise you have completed.

Daily Exercises

DAYS OF THE WEEK

	SU	M	T	W	T	F	S
MORNING GROUNDING							
Meditation	○	○	○	○	○	○	○
Journaling	○	○	○	○	○	○	○
EVENING REFLECTION	○	○	○	○	○	○	○

Self-Devotional Practices

	SU	M	T	W	T	F	S
MOVEMENT _____	○	○	○	○	○	○	○
NOURISHMENT _____	○	○	○	○	○	○	○
YOUR OWN DEVOTION _____	○	○	○	○	○	○	○

Notes

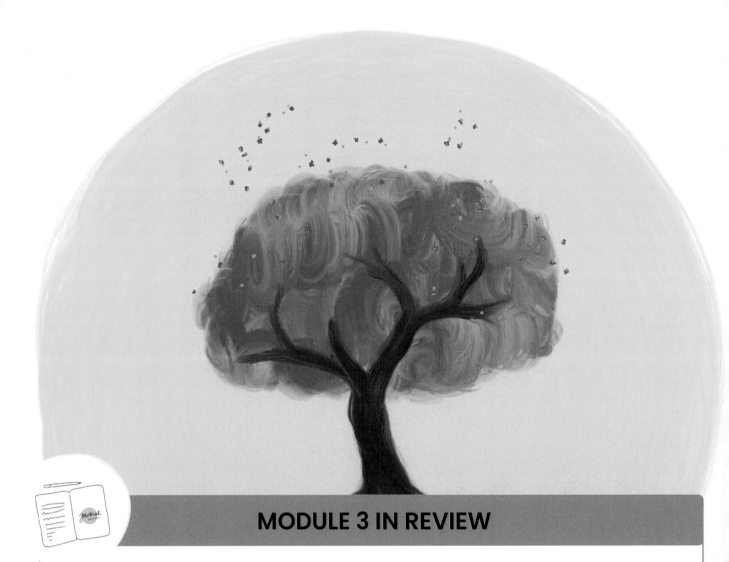

MODULE 3 IN REVIEW

Without judgment, review your weekly tracker. How many days were you able to implement your self-devotional practices? How can you adjust them for the week ahead?

Reflecting back on the past month, what are your top learnings from this module?

Looking back to where you started when you opened this workbook, what has changed for you? What are some of the highlights of your experience from the past 12 weeks?

Knowing what you know now, which practices do you plan to carry forward?

LOOKING FORWARD

CONGRATULATIONS!

You have completed the Choose Yourself 12-week journey! While creating this workbook, it was my greatest wish that it would act as a map and guidebook for what many have described as a life-long journey of self-love.

Now that you have finished this workbook, a couple of things may happen...

- There may be a magic moment when your daily practice becomes essential.

- Folks may ask you how you can "possibly" meditate everyday.

- You secretly wonder why other people *can't* meditate everyday - it has somehow become that important to your well-being.

- Or, you may drift away from your practices - after all, life provides us with a myriad of distractions. Awesome, too!

So, if you find yourself revisiting sections of this workbook, that is by design. There are an infinite number of layers of "self" to process. Celebrate the moments when your grounding and journaling practices reveal new insights and perspectives. Rejoice in the seemingly never ending well of answers your spirit provides in your moments of stillness. Delight yourself in the ever-increasing intimacy that builds between you and your higher self. No judgment necessary!

I will never forget something a former therapist once told me. Life is like a grand, spiral staircase and sometimes, we just *think* we are standing in the same spot. In all actuality, we are standing on a much higher level, viewing that familiar spot with a heightened understanding and increased awareness.

When moments of insecurity, self-criticism or self-judgment emerge - as they often will - turn your face towards the sun. Immerse yourself in self-devotion. Remind yourself that there is no finish line - there is simply the continual unfoldment that is YOU.

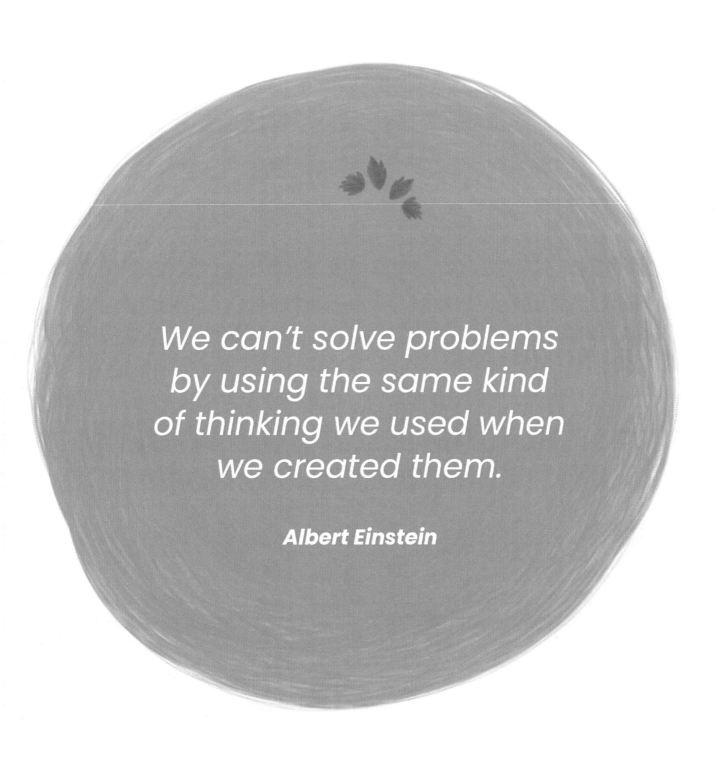

*We can't solve problems
by using the same kind
of thinking we used when
we created them.*

Albert Einstein

APPENDIX

All The "Feels"

ALL THE "FEELS"

I once heard that "feelings aren't facts" - but that doesn't make them any less real. Sometimes, it can be tricky to put a name to what we are feeling. This list of a few "feels" should steer you in the right direction.

A
Adored
Apprehensive
Agitated
Awe
Apathetic
Appreciated
Alienated
Amused
Angry
Aroused
Aggravated
Alive
Amazed
Annoyed
Anxious
Abandoned

B
Bored
Baffled
Brooding
Beautiful
Bitter
Bubbly

C
Calm
Curious
Creative
Compassionate
Cozy
Courageous
Content
Confident
Carefree
Clear
Contemplative

Cheerful
Critical
Comfortable

D
Decisive
Disappointed
Delighted
Discouraged
Defeated
Devoted
Doubtful
Daring
Depressed
Driven
Dedicated
Dazzled

E
Eager
Energized
Empathetic
Excited
Envious
Embarrassed
Exasperated
Effervescent
Excluded
Ecstatic
Encouraged
Enamored

F
Fulfilled
Fearful
Fanciful
Frustrated
Fruitful

Furious
Fantastic
Fragile
Faith-Filled

G
Graceful
Gleeful
Guilty
Grateful
Grief-Stricken
Glum
Glad
Generous
Grounded

H
Happy
Harmonious
Hurt
Helpless
Humiliated
Hopeful
Hungry

I
Inspired
Inquisitive
Imaginative
Isolated
Intuitive
Indignant
Inadequate
Interested
Indifferent
Insistent
Insecure

J
Joyous
Jaded
Judgmental
Jealous
Jubilant

K
Knowledgeable
Kind
Kid-Like

L
Loving
Lonely
Listless
Lustful
Longing
Luminous

M
Masterful
Mundane
Melancholy
Merciful
Miserable
Meticulous
Magnanimous
Mad

N
Nervous
Nostalgic
Numb
Nice

O
Optimistic
Opulent
Oppositional
Observant
Overwhelmed

P
Pressured
Proud
Positive
Passionate
Peaceful
Present
Provoked
Playful
Powerful
Panicked
Patient

Q
Quiet
Quick (witted/minded)

R
Rested
Ridiculed
Rageful
Relaxed
Resistant
Resentful
Radiant
Relieved
Remorseful
Romantic

S
Sensual
Sexy
Shy
Sad
Satisfied
Shameful
Sensitive
Stressed
Satiated
Stimulated
Strong
Self-Assured

T
Tense
Thrilled
Tethered
Tantalized
Threatened
Trusting
Thoughtful

U
Unbothered
Useful
Unified

V
Vulnerable
Vital
Vibrant
Validated

W
Worked (over)
Wilted
Wonderful
Wonder-Filled
Wild
Worried
Warmhearted
Wanderlusty

Y
Yearning

Z
Zealous
Zesty

Terms

TERMS

Agreement: An unconscious or conscious pact between you and another person, place or thing.

Amusement: An energetic posture of observation which can dissolve resistance, attachment to or judgment of what is being observed.

Body Of Glass: A metaphor that represents an illumined state, free from triggers and therefore, free from reactivity.

Codependent: To be extremely attached to another individual and/or overly reliant on another for your emotional and psychological well-being; may be accompanied by an impulsive urge to fix, save or heal that person.

Core Needs: The fundamental wants, desires and/or necessities required to survive and to facilitate emotional, psychological and/or physical wellbeing.

Cosmic Energy: A neutral and validating energy that compliments the grounding aspect of your meditation by providing its counterpart (earth + sky); a visual tool that allows you to connect with the cosmos.

Emotional Regulation: The ability to feel emotions fully without numbing, self-medicating or bypassing, thus allowing oneself to move seamlessly from one feeling to another, allowing you to gain dominion over your emotional states; accepting of emotional states (Psychology Today).

Energy Vampire: An individual who feeds off the energy of others in order to manipulate, gain control or for other egoic purposes. This person may also drain another's energy in an effort to regulate their own nervous system.

Energetic Boundary: The edge of your human energetic field or aura; an intentional line of demarcation that can be asserted to protect your sense of self and distinguish your thoughts, feelings and emotions from those of another's.

Golden Sun: A visual tool to revitalize, self-validate or recharge; utilized to seal or close your grounding meditation.

Grounding: Connecting to the earth and its qualities through physical contact (ex: earthing), practices or visualizations; can be used to orient oneself to the present moment, thus releasing anxiety and assisting in the regulation of the nervous system.

Grounding Cord: A subjective visual tool connecting the root chakra or base of spine to the center of the earth; a grounding tool.

Meditation: To engage in mental exercise (such as concentration on one's breathing or repetition of a mantra) for the purpose of reaching a heightened level of spiritual awareness (Merriam-Webster). Other examples include walking meditation, grounding meditation, breathwork, body scanning or sound meditation.

Object Constancy: A cognitive skill developed in early childhood that allows you to feel a sense of safety within, independent of the presence of a parent, partner, job, etc (American Psychological Association).

Perch: This is your sanctuary, your place of power and authority, visually represented in the center of mind, behind the eyes; third eye.

Point Of Focus: A meditative posture that centers on a specific visualization, such as a tree, flower, the sky, a flame, etc.; can be used as a tool to steady the mind and promote awareness of the present moment.

Relational Trauma: A term used to describe the aftermath of abuse, neglect, maltreatment, or abandonment within a relationship (Tanasugarn).

Ruminating: Fixating or spiraling on a thought or group of thoughts related to the past ("I should've") or future ("what if") events; when unchecked, can lead to depression or anxiety.

Self-Devotional Practices: Curated and customized self-care practices that directly or indirectly meet your core needs.

Shadow: Specific features of an individual's psyche that they block, repress, or defend against because the material is both threatening and seen as antithetical to what they wish they were (Henriques and Madison).

Dedication

*For mom, who always dared me to be different.
Your unwavering belief in me has been my rock,
in many storms.*

Made in the USA
Las Vegas, NV
17 October 2024